INDIA

TITLES IN THE MODERN NATIONS OF THE WORLD SERIES INCLUDE:

Brazil
Canada
China
Cuba
Egypt
England
Germany
Greece
India
Ireland
Italy
Japan
Kenya
Mexico
Russia
Somalia
South Africa
South Korea
Spain
Sweden
The United States

INDIA

BY WILLIAM GOODWIN

LUCENT BOOKS
P.O. BOX 289011
SAN DIEGO, CA 92198-9011

Dedicated to the memory of Mahatma Gandhi

Library of Congress Cataloging-in-Publication Data

Goodwin, William, 1943–
    India / by William Goodwin.
       p.   cm. — (Modern nations of the world)
    Includes bibliographical references and index.
    Summary: Discusses the geography, climate, history, government,
spiritual and ethnic diversity, arts, culture, complexities, and challenges
of India.
    ISBN 1-56006-598-2 (lib. : alk. paper)
    1. India Juvenile literature. 2. India—History—20th century Juvenile
literature.   [1. India.] I. Title.   II. Series.
DS407.G65 2000
954—dc21
                                    99-40501
                                        CIP

Copyright © 2000 by Lucent Books, Inc.
P.O. Box 289011, San Diego, CA 92198-9011
Printed in the U.S.A.

CONTENTS

INTRODUCTION

INDIA: "LAND OF WONDERS"

The Greeks, who were the first Europeans to visit India, described the region's wonders in the third century B.C. Throughout the intervening centuries, India has continued to inspire wonder in all who travel to this vast and diverse country. After the American writer Mark Twain visited India in 1896, he admitted to being so awed by the country that he was almost speechless. Usually a man of many words, in this case Twain stated, "I can not conjure the phrases to adequately describe the worlds within worlds of this vast land, so forgive me if I say only that India is the Land of Wonders."[1]

To say India is diverse is inadequate. India is astoundingly diverse. Medieval village life exists in the shadows of nuclear power plants. Elephants serenely wade on the tropical shores of rivers fed from glaciers deep in the world's highest mountain range. Hindu priests practice the oldest living religion while scientists design state-of-the-art satellites. The people and the land of India are almost indescribably diverse. India has an ethnically, culturally, and spiritually differentiated population of about 1 billion, one-sixth of the world's population. These people live in an area one-third the size of the United States that has tall mountain ranges, steaming jungles, immense rivers, lush farmlands, great plains and deltas, and shores on two seas. Indians speak more than a dozen major languages and over a thousand different dialects. India is the world's largest democracy with more than twenty political parties, a reflection of the extremely diverse cultures based on historical foundations going back more than four millennia.

India's immense social diversity is matched by its geographical diversity. Parts of the world's highest mountain range crown the northern limits of the country, and the Indian Ocean and Arabian Sea surround it on two sides. Between the peaks and the sea, many large rivers wind their way through fertile plains, plateaus, and smaller mountain ranges. In the west, the Great Indian Desert receives almost no moisture while most of the rest of the country is green with lush tropical growth. India is blessed with rich soils and abundant water. All this fertility made it possible for civilization to bloom early here, and India's early civilizations were at least as advanced as other contemporary cultures in Mesopotamia, Greece, and Egypt.

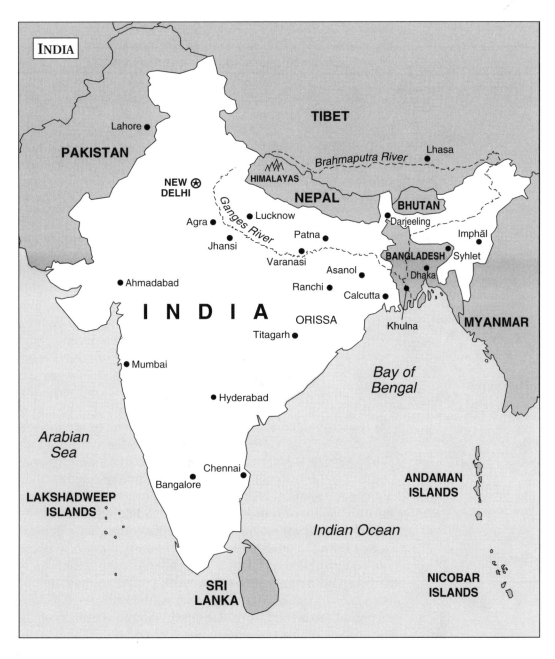

The beginning of the twenty-first century finds India in a position to become one of the world's great powers. Besides having the fifth largest economy in the world, India has a well-educated and affluent middle class that is almost as large as the entire U.S. population. India has built fast-paced, high-tech industries that launch communications satellites with Indian-made rockets, produce over fifty cable television channels, and meet much of the nation's energy require-ments with nuclear power plants. India recently joined the exclusive club of the major military powers of the world by demonstrating that it has functional nuclear weapons.

Children abound in a nation known for its high birthrate and rapidly growing pop-ulation.

The growth in India's middle class and the strength of the national economy does not mean all is well in this ancient and crowded land. India continues to be plagued by high unemployment, over-crowding, illiteracy, and one of the world's lowest per capita incomes. Most of these problems can be traced directly to the ex-tremely high rate at which the population is growing. If current population trends continue, by the middle of the twenty-first century India will be the most populous country on the planet. While family plan-ning and other national programs have succeeded in reducing births from 6.0 children per woman in 1950 to 3.4 in 1998, the death rate has dropped due to better health care helping Indians to live longer. Consequently the struggle continues to accommodate over a million more people every month. With a growth rate like this, India has a greater struggle than many other countries in its efforts to become a thoroughly modern nation.

More than half a century after India gained its indepen-dence from Great Britain, the nation continues to struggle with diverse political and cultural forces that tug it in many different directions. Throughout history India's diversity has both helped and hindered it, and now the leaders of this an-cient and modern country are striving to make this diversity the engine of renewed greatness.

Geographical, Climatic, and Biological Diversity

The land now known as India looked quite different 150 million years ago than it does today. Then India was a continent-sized island located in the Indian Ocean below the vast expanse of Asia. This island-India was, and still is, a part of the earth's crust called a tectonic plate. The diamond-shaped tectonic plate under India was slowly moving northward, and when it eventually collided with the unmovable mass of Asia, island-India became a subcontinent. The tectonic plate under the Indian subcontinent, however, did not stop moving, and even today it continues to jam up against China. The earthquakes that occur frequently in the regions south of the Himalayas are evidence that the subcontinent continues to grind against and slip under Asia.

Where India meets Asia, the land has buckled, folded, and tilted up to form the Himalayan mountain range, the tallest mountain range in the world. The eye-catching height and length of these mountains makes them the obvious starting point for a study of India's geographical features. The Himalayas are so massive that they are directly responsible for much of the weather patterns on the subcontinent. For months each year, huge moisture-filled weather systems called monsoons blow up from the Indian Ocean. Blocked by the wall of the Himalayan mountains, the monsoons are trapped into depositing their heavy rains on the subcontinent.

The monsoons strike the southern tip of India first, pass over the lesser mountains known as the Western and Eastern Ghats, and finally are stopped by the southern slopes of Himalayan peaks. Several great river systems drain the abundant rain that falls from the monsoons, and the valleys and plains through which these rivers flow are some of the most

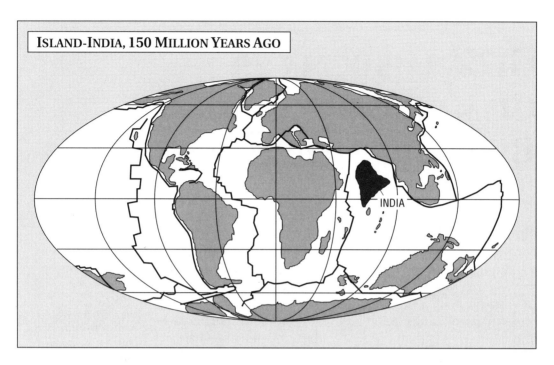

ISLAND-INDIA, 150 MILLION YEARS AGO

INDIA

fertile lands on earth. In addition to the mountain ranges, plains, plateaus, valleys, and tropical forests where the monsoons bring plentiful rain, India also has arid, sparsely populated places where little rain falls.

In many ways life in India reflects the subcontinent's geographical and climatic diversity—within the boundaries of one country are harsh deserts, glaciers, and eternal snows in some of the world's highest mountains, steamy jungles where tigers still roam, one of the wettest places on earth, some of the most fertile lowlands on the planet, and gracefully terraced highlands where tea and rice grow.

A CRUCIAL LOCATION

The modern nation of India, officially known as the Republic of India, lies across the tropic of Cancer in southern Asia. The territory of India occupies most of the diamond-shaped subcontinent and includes several groups of islands in the Bay of Bengal and the Arabian Sea. In total area (1.27 million square miles), India is Asia's second largest country (after China) and about one-third the size of the United States.

India's neighbors are Pakistan to the northwest, China and Nepal to the north and northeast, Bhutan, Bangladesh (formerly East Pakistan), and Myanmar (formerly Burma) to the east, and Sri Lanka (formerly Ceylon), which is an hour's boat ride across a narrow strait from the southeast tip of India.

The Indian subcontinent may be divided into four relatively well-defined geographical regions: the Himalaya Mountains, the northern plains of the Ganges River and its tributaries (the Gangetic Plain), the southern plateau (the Deccan), bordered by ranges of hills and lesser mountains (Eastern and Western Ghats), and the northwestern desert area (the Thar Desert). Besides these continental regions, India also has three groups of oceanic islands.

THE GREATEST MOUNTAIN CHAIN ON EARTH

The Himalayan mountains in the far north of the country are the mightiest mountains in the world. Because of their height and length, this greatest of all mountain ranges forms an imposing physical barrier between India and China. No other range has mountains higher than twenty-three thousand feet above sea level, but fourteen Himalayan peaks are over twenty-six thousand feet and hundreds of them are over

Mount Kachenjunga, the third highest mountain on earth, is located in the mighty Himalaya Mountains, which border northern India.

twenty-three thousand. While much of this immense mountain chain is located in Nepal, China, Bhutan, and Pakistan, some of the tallest mountains are also located within India's borders. The tallest peak located at least partially within India is Kanchenjunga (28,208 feet), the third highest mountain on earth (after Mount Everest in Nepal and K2 in Pakistan).

Much of the rock comprising the Himalayan mountains was once under water, part of a vast shallow sea that lay between present-day China and India. Limestone rocks bearing marine fossils are found at the tops of some of the highest peaks. Because of continuing pressure from the tectonic plates, the Himalayas are still growing at a rate of about thirty feet every hundred years.

Indian territory includes two quite distinct parts of the Himalayas. Kanchenjunga is located in the eastern Himalayan ranges in the Indian territory of Sikkim, a region known for its icy ruggedness. To the west between Nepal, Pakistan, and China rise India's Garhwal Himalayas, often called the loveliest of all the mountains in central Asia. Many Hindu and Buddhist holy sites are found in the lush, harmonious settings of the region's mountains and valleys.

Below the Garhwal Himalayas is Kashmir, a fertile valley of an almost dreamlike natural beauty. Because Kashmir and other places near the Himalayan slopes are cool in the summer, resorts known as "hill stations" provide an escape for many Indians from the relentless heat of the plains. A danger in the Himalayan mountains is the frequent earthquakes that occur near these geologically young formations. From time to time earthquakes cause extensive damage in the densely populated sub-Himalayan valleys and plains.

GREAT RIVERS FLOW FROM GREAT MOUNTAINS

All of India's largest rivers, including the Indus (located mostly in present-day Pakistan), Ganges (also called Ganga), Yamuna (also called Jumna), and Brahmaputra, have their sources in the great snowfields and glaciers of the Himalayan mountains. During and after the monsoons, these rivers roar down the steep gorges, flowing fast and eroding rock as they go. As a result of this extensive erosion, vast quantities of silt are suspended in the rushing mountain waters. Then when the water reaches the relative flatness of the plains, the rivers slow and deposit their loads of silt and minerals to create rich new soil. This yearly replenishment and enrichment has made India's northern river plains some of the most fertile farmlands in the world.

The two most important rivers in India are the Ganges and the Brahmaputra. Ganga Mai (Mother Ganges), India's most sacred river, is worshipped as a goddess by Hindus. The Ganges originates in the southern Himalayan mountains and drains a quarter of the Indian landmass before emptying into the Bay of Bengal. The Gangetic Plain, India's fertile heartland and home to a long series of major civilizations, is a creation of the Ganges and her tributaries.

The Yamuna River flows past Agra, where its waters reflect the gleaming Taj Mahal before merging with the Ganges at Allahabad. Other lesser rivers join the Ganges at frequent intervals, yet despite its volume, the river's length of 1,557 miles makes it only the fifteenth longest river in Asia and the thirty-ninth longest in the world. The Brahmaputra is longer, flowing 1,800 miles from its source in the Tibetan Himalayas to where it joins the Ganges in Bangladesh. Together, these two great rivers form a vast delta that covers much of northeastern India and most of Bangladesh. The floodplain formed by the Ganges and Brahmaputra contains some of the most agriculturally productive soil in the world.

The Indus River arises in the Himalayan mountains near the Indian region of Ladakh and flows through the states of

Boats pull away from the bank of the Brahmaputra River. The rivers of India play a crucial role in the country's agriculture.

DOLPHINS IN THE GANGES

The Ganges is the holiest river to Hindus, and the most holy city on the Ganges is named Varanasi. All lanes of this ancient city seem to end at the river where wide steps called ghats (like the mountains) lead down into the brown waters of the Ganges. Every year hundreds of thousands of people are cremated on the ghats and their ashes scattered into the river. The Ganges also flows through many large cities and industrial areas. The water may look polluted, it may test polluted, but to devout Hindus, to bathe in the Ganges is to be cleansed of sin.

Humans are not the only mammals who use the Ganges. The Ganges River dolphins, found only in the Ganges, Brahmaputra, and other nearby rivers, never go into the sea. Like dolphins everywhere, they use echo location (biological sonar) to feed and to "visualize" their surroundings. In the case of these river dolphins, echo location literally takes the place of sight because their eyes are lensless and underdeveloped. They can sense only light and dark, which is just as well because the rivers are so murky. These dolphins often swim on their sides in shallow water, one fin touching the bottom, while their tail moves from side to side. The World Wildlife Federation estimates that fewer than two thousand Ganges River dolphins survive.

A crowd gathers at the Ganges River, which is sacred to Hindus.

Jammu and Kashmir, but for most of its length of 1,800 miles it flows southward through present-day Pakistan. The fertile Indus Valley nurtured some of the subcontinent's earliest civilizations, and its name is the origin of the word "India."

DESERTS, PLATEAUS, GHATS, AND ISLANDS

The province of Punjab in northwestern India is centered between five other important rivers that flow from the Himalayan mountains. These rivers, shared by India and Pakistan, are the Jhelum, the Chenab, the Ravi, the Beas, and the Sutlej. The name "Punjab" comes from *panch ab,* meaning five waters.

Because of the directions from which the monsoons sweep into India, the most western sector of the country, particularly the state of Rajasthan and the surrounding area, receives very little rain. Consequently this region, consisting mostly of the Thar Desert, is the most arid part of India.

Running across the center of the country, the Vindhya Mountains and the Narmada River form a natural boundary between the

A man leads a camel through the Thar Desert of western India.

northern and southern parts of India. Below this line, the southern half of the Indian subcontinent is a broad central flatland known as the Deccan Plateau. The Deccan is more or less framed on each side with relatively low mountains called ghats. The Western Ghats run parallel to the coast of the Arabian Sea and close to shore; the Eastern Ghats are farther inland, leaving a broad coastal plain along the southeast coast of the Bay of Bengal. The Arabian Sea and the Bay of Bengal stretch southward to join the Indian Ocean.

India's territory also includes three groups of offshore islands. Far out in the Bay of Bengal to the east, closer to Indonesia than they are to the subcontinent, are India's Andaman and Nicobar Islands. Offshore from the southwestern coast of India in the Arabian Sea are the Lakshadweep Islands. All of these islands are tropical in character, surrounded by coral reefs and warm water.

VEGETATION

India has a distinct identity not only because of its geography, history, and culture but also because of the great diversity of its natural ecosystems. About a third of all India's plants are endemic (native), a particularly high figure when compared to other large countries. About 45,000 species of plants are found in India. As one of the oldest and largest agricultural societies, India also has an impressive variety of at least 166 species of crop plants and 320 species of wild relatives of cultivated crops.

Botanists have identified sixteen major types of forests in India, which cover roughly one-fifth of the country's land area. These range from evergreen tropical rain forests in the Andaman and Nicobar Islands, the Western Ghats, and the northeastern states, to dry alpine scrub high in the Himalayan mountains. Between these two extremes, the country's varied ecological systems support the growth of semievergreen rain forests, deciduous monsoon forests, thorn forests, subtropical pine forests, and temperate mountain forests.

The three main regions where tropical forests are found are in the Andaman and Nicobar Islands, the Western Ghats, and the Assam region in the northeast. These three tropical forest zones differ in species and plant distribution, and all are negatively affected by human activities. Expanding needs for farmland and heavy logging place the remaining forests at risk of being reduced to isolated remnants like the little patches of rain forest still found in the densely populated state of Orissa (south of Calcutta).

India's beautiful tropical rain forests are one example of the country's diverse terrain.

The Western Ghats contain several species of trees that have great commercial value, most notably rosewood and teak. In most areas of these mountains, however, uncontrolled logging has drastically reduced the forests. Often where forests have been clear-cut by loggers, the valleys and hillsides become overgrown with bamboo thickets.

In northeastern India (including the states of Assam, Nagaland, Manipur, Mizoram, Tripura, and Meghalaya), dense tropical vegetation grows from sea level up to about twenty-seven hundred feet. This junglelike growth is made up mostly of evergreen and semievergreen rain forests, deciduous monsoon forests (green following the monsoon rains), riparian forests (growing on river and lake shores), swamps, and grasslands.

The Andaman and Nicobar Islands have tall tropical evergreen and semievergreen rain forests as well as monsoon forests. Even though these forests grow on oceanic islands, they are only slightly less grand in size and number of species than the forests on the Indian mainland.

Regions of India that are heavily populated have little forest remaining. The Gangetic Plain is almost entirely under cultivation with a wide variety of crops and has very little wild growth. The Deccan Plateau is also heavily farmed, but there are large regions of scrub and deciduous forests where no farming occurs.

ANIMALS

India has been identified as one of the world's twelve megacenters of biological diversity. In addition to the 45,000 species of plants found here, there are 8,100 species of animals including 396 species of mammals, 1,228 species of birds, 446 species of reptiles, and 204 species of amphibians. Only 3 percent of the mammals are native to India while 14 percent of the birds, 32 percent of the reptiles, and 62 percent of the amphibians are endemic.

While the population of large mammals is not as diverse or as numerous as Africa's, India is home to sizeable wild populations of the Asian elephant, tiger, one-horned rhinoceros, Asiatic lion, panther, wild buffalo, leopard, tapir, mountain sheep, antelope, and deer. Thanks to a vigorous protection program, India's tiger population, less than two thousand in 1972, is now back up to almost four thousand individuals.

Many species of monkeys and other primates live in India. By far the most common are the rhesus monkeys, which carry

CORBETT NATIONAL PARK: FROM HUNTING TO PROTECTING TIGERS

Early in the twentieth century, a man-eating tiger was terrorizing villages in a remote region of northern India. The tiger would lurk about the village until it spotted a person walking alone, and then it would attack. Repeated efforts by local officials to capture or kill the tiger failed. Then a well-known British hunter, Jim Corbett, heard about this tiger and went to the village. After tracking the elusive man-eater, he found and shot it.

A few decades later, the number of Indian tigers had declined as a result of hunting and loss of habitat as forests were replaced by farms. Instead of hunting tigers, Indian environmentalists worried about the possibility that the country's big cats were becoming extinct. As a result, the Indian government began designating special preserves where tigers could be protected. Among those preserves was Corbett National Park, near the area where the man-eater had been killed. In recent years India's Project Tiger has expanded the tiger preserves in several parts of India.

Endangered tigers find a haven in one of the many reserves founded for their protection.

on their lives right in the middle of many human settlements and often boldly compete with people for food and space.

Because of overhunting and the loss of habitat, crocodiles and gharials (a type of crocodile unique to India), which were once abundant, are now near extinction. Other Indian reptiles include cobras, sea snakes, and pythons.

Bird life is abundant and includes pheasants, mynahs, parakeets, hornbills, storks, ibises, cranes, spoonbills, kingfishers, and the spectacular Indian peafowl, the national bird.

The nearshore coastal waters of India are extremely rich fishing grounds, and Indian commercial fisheries catch about 1.5 million tons of fish each year. Five species of marine turtles are also found in Indian waters, but their numbers have declined drastically in recent years.

Even though seawater temperatures are easily warm enough for coral to grow, reefs occur along only a few sections of India's coastline. This is because there are so many rivers carrying sediment and freshwater into coastal waters that would otherwise support abundant coral growth. On the other hand, extensive coral reefs are found in the Andaman, Nicobar, and Lakshadweep Islands, which are far enough offshore not to be affected by rivers.

The wildlife of the Indian subcontinent has remained unique, mysterious, and fascinating to nature lovers. For Hindus, life in any form is sacred, and compassion for all animals is a basic element of their religion. Environmentalists, international wildlife groups, and India's own people have united to help preserve the subcontinent's unique and vital flora and fauna. Since independence in 1947, the Indian government has established seventy national parks and over four hundred sanctuaries.

CLIMATE

The Himalayan mountains isolate the subcontinent from the rest of Asia, which results in a climate that is, like India's terrain, diverse and different from the rest of Asia. Many climatologists have called India's weather violent because of the suddenness with which it changes and the intensity of its effects. An example is the way the monsoon rains typically start: Into a clear blue sky above the parched country, huge clouds suddenly appear. Accompanied by powerful winds, the clouds release torrential downpours that immediately bring widespread flooding, rapid erosion, and great fluctuations in temperature and wind.

Though it seems that most of the time India is either hot and dry or hot and flooded, in fact the country's climate consists of four distinct seasons. These are described by the Indian Meteorological Service as the relatively dry winter, with winds from the north bringing cooler temperatures (December through February); the dry summer (March through May) when the country becomes very hot and no rain falls; the southwest monsoon (arriving in late May or early June and lasting until October) with great storm clouds sweeping in from the Arabian Sea with torrential rains; and the retreating monsoon (October and November) that brings more rain from the northeast.

THE INDIAN COBRA

Cobras are highly poisonous snakes best known for their fascinating neck-hoods and as the subject of snake charmers. The Indian cobra grows up to 5.5 feet long. Cobras cause several hundred deaths each year. This is at least partly due to the way cobras are accepted in the midst of human habitation. According to India expert Stanley Wolpert, "Households blessed with a cobra family in residence seldom complain, since those regal hooded snakes are considered good luck for childbearing women. . . . [E]very Indian child learns early in life never to reach under a tablecloth or into any dark closet."

The Indian cobra has an especially wide hood, made by expanding its ribs, which it uses to frighten prey and enemies. Snake charmers tease cobras to coax them into an upright, hood-expanded position. The charmers use swaying movements and other motions to tempt the snake to move with them in preparation for striking. Contrary to popular conception, cobras do not respond to the sound of the horn—they are deaf to high frequencies. The successful snake charmer never takes his eyes off the snake because he must be constantly on the watch for a strike, which can be avoided by a fast charmer because the cobra's lunge is relatively slow.

A snake charmer coaxes his cobra into an upright position.

The monsoons are the most dramatic weather feature of the subcontinent. These rains spell the difference between life and death in many parts of India. The monsoons arrive first at the bottom of the subcontinent, hitting the south of India around the end of May, and gradually move northward. People in the state of Kashmir in the extreme northwest of the country may not receive the monsoon's first rains until July. In normal years most of the country receives monsoon rains for about three months. Each day during that time, the sky opens and a deluge soaks the fields, swells the rivers, temporarily floods villages and cities alike, and then stops. The sun comes out and everything steams for a few hours until the rain starts again. As the monsoons continue, rivers that a few weeks before could be easily crossed simply by wading from one bank to the other become broad, raging torrents.

The monsoons always bring abundant rain to southwestern India, so the Western Ghats and coastal states like Kerala are lush and green all year as a result. But in some years the monsoon fails to reach the northwestern areas of the country, which has disastrous consequences for the farmers. In the Thar Desert, it is not unheard of for eighteen months to pass without a drop of rain falling. Whenever the monsoon fails, crops die for lack of water and large numbers of people and animals face starvation. On the other hand, monsoon rains often cause flash floods capable of sweeping away entire villages and drowning many humans and animals.

CITIES

Even though three quarters of the people in India live in villages, about 500 million people live in cities. There are twenty-two Indian cities with populations over 1 million, and of these, seven are truly immense.

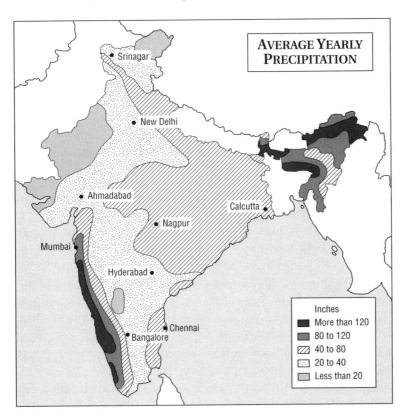

Once one of the richest shopping districts in the world, the bustling Chandi Chowk is representative of Old Delhi city life.

The largest and most densely populated Indian city is Calcutta in the northeast state of Bengal. Calcutta, the former capital of the British Raj, was designed for no more than 2.5 million people but is now home to over 12 million.

India's second largest city is Mumbai, formerly Bombay. Mumbai is located on the west coast and is known as the gateway to India. This city in the west of India is the business capital of the country and the biggest film producing city in the world.

New Delhi, the capital of India and its third-largest city, consists of Old Delhi and New Delhi. Old Delhi grew up in the seventeenth century and has the city gates, crowded bazaars, and narrow streets to prove it. New Delhi is a planned city of wide, tree-lined streets running through modern business, governmental, and residential areas.

Bangalore is the capital of the south-central Indian state of Karnataka. With a population of approximately 6 million, Bangalore is one of the fastest-growing cities in the world. It has a world-class software industry—some call it the "Silicon Valley of India." The city is also known for its fashion and electronics industries.

Chennai, previously known as Madras, is the capital of the south Indian state of Tamil Nadu. This city of over 5 million is a modern seaport with ancient Dravidian roots.

Ahmedabad is capital of Gujarat state in the west of India. This city of 4.8 million is a textile and commercial center and the second most important city in the west (after Mumbai).

Hyderabad is the capital of the state of Andhra Pradesh, with a population of about 4.2 million.

Roots: Three Thousand Years of Indian Civilization

The Republic of India is a very young nation—it has existed only since 1947. But Indian civilization has roots that go back more than forty-five hundred years. Even during prehistoric times, there were people living in the area that is now called India.

The Indian subcontinent, which includes India, Pakistan, and Bangladesh, has been home to many complex and advanced cultures. Human civilizations flourished in the subcontinent at least as far back as the earliest civilizations in Europe (Greece and other places), the Middle East (Sumeria and Babylonia), and North Africa (Egypt).

People living in India knew about these civilizations as early as the third millennium B.C., and there are convincing reasons to believe that these different cultures exchanged ideas about religion, mathematics, and language. Yet extensive evidence from archeological sites along the fertile Indus Valley in present-day Pakistan and other locations in western India prove that although the early inhabitants of the subcontinent traded with Egypt, Greece, and Sumeria, their cultures developed independently.

THE INDUS VALLEY CIVILIZATION

By 2500 B.C. the Indian subcontinent was home to planned cities that supported advanced agricultural practices, economic structures, mathematics, literature, and arts. The earliest well-developed civilization in India is known as the Indus Valley civilization. Named for the Indus River, where the first cities of this ancient culture were discovered in the 1920s, this civilization extended over a much larger area than contemporary civilizations along the Nile in Egypt and along

23

the Tigris and Euphrates Rivers in Mesopotamia. Recent archaeological excavations have determined that the Indus Valley civilization covered an area larger than Western Europe. The ruins of cities and villages from this civilization have been discovered throughout northwestern India (917 sites, many along a river that no longer exists) as well as along the Indus in Pakistan (481 sites).

The Indus Valley civilization began around 2500 B.C. when cities began to rise among the scattered agricultural settlements that had existed there for many centuries. The people who built this civilization were Dravidians, a culture whose roots are lost in prehistory. The descendants of India's original Dravidian people currently comprise a large percentage of the population in south India. The most thoroughly studied of the ancient Dravidian cities are Mohenjo Daro and Harappa, now in ruins in the Indus Valley. These cities contained street layouts and building designs at least as advanced as anywhere else in the world at the time. Viewed from above, Dravidian cities always formed a parallelogram. Structures were built of bricks that were always made with exactly the same dimensions. All their cities used the same system of weights and measures. These consistencies indicate that this culture was united under a central government, although there is no archeological evidence of what kind of government that might have been.

The Dravidians also kept accounting records and had a written language. They used a distinctive script that had 419 symbols, a script that has never been deciphered.

The ruins of the city of Mohenjo Daro have given researchers insight into the lives of ancient Indian civilizations.

The Indus Valley civilization flourished for almost a thousand years, and then in a relatively brief span of time it disappeared. No one knows for sure what happened, although some believe the rain failed for many years or that earthquakes destroyed the brick buildings. Others believe that when Aryan nomads from central Asia invaded, they drove the Dravidians out. Whether it happened violently or peacefully, by 1500 B.C., the lighter-skinned Aryans had replaced the dark-skinned Dravidians in northern India, and the Dravidians had migrated to the south of the subcontinent.

THE ARYANS AND THE VEDAS

The Aryans came to India from the grasslands of central Asia, probably around the Caspian Sea. They were nomadic cattle-herders who left very little behind to reveal their history. No Aryan cities, sculpture, pottery, or burial grounds have been found, but they did leave four books of verse called the Vedas. These books provide strong evidence of the Aryans' five hundred years of domination in India. In Sanskrit, the ancient language of south Asia, the word *veda* means "knowledge," and the Vedas, considered to be some of the oldest religious writings, were the repository of all Aryan knowledge at the time.

Forming the foundations of Hinduism, the Vedas are a mixture of history and religious teachings. Filled with epic stories written mostly in verse, the Vedas tell how the Aryans lived and how the gods made the universe. They also tell about the organization of Aryan society, sacrifices to the gods, battles between different tribes, and battles between different gods. To this day Hindu priests chant hymns from the Vedas during ceremonies in homes and temples. In the centuries after the appearance of the Vedas, other epic tales like the *Ramayana* and the *Mahabharata* were added to the body of Hindu scripture in keeping with the tradition of a perpetually evolving religion.

The Aryans introduced a system of social divisions consisting of nobles, priests, warriors, and ordinary people. As time passed, the religion and society of the Aryans gradually evolved into the enormous complexity of Hinduism and the Indian class, or caste, system. From the earliest times the priests, known as Brahmins, held the highest position in the caste system. This had two important effects on the future of Indian society. First, it attached a high value to spiritual and philosophical thinking. Second, the lower castes began to seek a different religious structure that would not exclude them. These two factors combined in the sixth century B.C. to aid the spread of India's second great contribution to the world's religions, Buddhism, which offered its devotees a path to religious enlightenment without regard to caste.

MORE INVASIONS FROM THE NORTHWEST

India has one of the oldest, most complex national histories of all the world's civilizations. For three millennia, from roughly 1500 B.C. to the beginning of the Mogul Empire around A.D. 1500, India's history is a dense tangle of rulers and kingdoms. Each new dynasty either collapsed upon itself because of internal fighting, was destroyed by rebellion, or was sacked by invaders.

King Darius I of Persia invaded India in 518 B.C. and added the Indus Valley and part of the Punjab in northwestern India to his vast Persian Empire. From the Aryans he demanded and received great wealth in the form of taxes. As a result, stories of great Indian treasures began to reach Europe. In 327 B.C., Alexander the Great of Macedonia overthrew Darius III and then continued east with the goal of conquering India. He met determined resistance, however, and quickly retreated from the subcontinent.

A Brahmin, or member of the highest caste.

THE MAURYAN EMPIRE

Following Alexander's defeat in northern India, and perhaps inspired by him, Chandragupta Maurya founded the first great Indian empire. By 300 B.C., he and his son Bindusara had established control over an area that ran from the mountains in northwestern India to the Bay of Bengal in the east. The highly organized state that Chandragupta and his successors created eventually extended as far south as the present-day state of Mysore. The Mauryan Empire is considered to be the first great Indian empire not only because of the extent of the empire's military and political control, but also because of the degree to which social organization, architecture, literature, and science advanced.

The seat of power of the Mauryan Empire was centered at the city of Patna on the Ganges River. The royal court existed in great splendor and luxury. Surviving paintings and hand-illustrated manuscripts from that time show the magnificent lifestyle of the Mauryan nobles and upper class. Detailed paintings show the nobility dressed in fine clothes and golden jewelry encrusted with diamonds, pearls, rubies, and sapphires. They also show large palaces that were elaborately decorated with carvings and inlaid with precious stones.

The Mauryan Empire reached its peak under Chandra-gupta's grandson, the extraordinary leader named Ashoka (272–236 B.C.). Many scholars assert that Ashoka was one of the greatest rulers the world has ever seen. Early in his career he fought brilliantly to enlarge the Mauryan Empire. Then after a particularly gruesome battle against an army from the Kalinga kingdom in west India, Ashoka, although victorious, was overcome with sadness. Seeing the slaughter and terrible suffering caused by the fighting, he had a change of heart. Within a few days, he became a Buddhist and adopted the Buddhist principle of ahimsa, the belief in nonviolence and the sacredness of all life. Ashoka gave up hunting, which at the time was considered the sport of kings, and became a vegetarian. He also changed the way he ruled, issuing decrees known today as Ashoka's Edicts. These laws sound surprisingly modern in seeking to establish harmony with the environment and to extend compassion and tolerance to

Sarnath, a major Buddhist center in Uttar Pradesh. After achieving enlightenment, Guttama Buddha visited Sarnath to preach his message of the middle way to Nirvana. Later, Ashoka, the great Buddhist emperor, erected the stupas. Dhamekh Stupa, the pillar that dominates the grounds, is said to be the exact site of the Buddha's famous sermon.

ALEXANDER THE GREAT IN INDIA

Alexander was a great military leader from Greece whose brief military excursion into India initiated the first exchange of ideas between the subcontinent and Europe. Through a string of bold military campaigns, Alexander conquered most of Mediterranean Europe, Egypt, Asia Minor, Syria, Mesopotamia, Persia, and Bactria (present-day Afghanistan), but India stopped him.

Alexander's army came up against warriors on elephants, a creature that most of the Greeks had never seen before. Nevertheless, Alexander's troops defeated the Indians in their first battle. Alexander's goal was to reach the Ganges River, but his troops had heard tales of the powerful Indian tribes that lived along the river, and the memory of their first difficult battle with the Indians was still fresh. They were also very far from home, and the troops finally refused to go any farther. Alexander had no choice but to build rafts and leave the subcontinent by floating down the Indus River to the coast, where they built ships for the return to Greek-controlled territory.

Alexander's brief visit had a lasting effect, however. From that exposure, Indian sculpture became more Greek-like. The cultural influence went both ways. Alexander was intrigued by the wisdom of the Hindu philosophers, called gurus, and at least one of these holy men accompanied the Greeks on their return home.

Alexander the Great was responsible for India's first contact with European culture.

people of different religions. One of the symbols of Ashoka's laws was the four-headed lion column, which became one of the major national emblems of modern India more than two thousand years after his death.

The spirit of Ashoka's rule is captured in this quotation from his writings: "All men are my children. As for my own children I desire that they may be provided with all the welfare and happiness of this world and of the next, so do I desire for all men as well."[2]

Ashoka's empire and his laws, however, did not last long after his death in 232 B.C., and he was the last of the Mauryan emperors. Within a few generations he was forgotten until his edicts were translated by archaeologists in 1837.

THE GUPTA EMPIRE

Following Ashoka's death, wave after wave of invaders poured into northern India from Asia. The Mauryan Empire disintegrated, and it would be more than five hundred years before India was again a unified kingdom.

During this half of a millennium, despite the divided and shifting political status of the country, India became one of the world's most important trading centers. Rome and other cities in Europe developed a great appetite for India's spices, drugs, sandalwood, cotton, silk, and precious stones. Europeans acquired these commodities by paying Indian merchants and princes in gold, wine, weapons, glass, and porcelain. Caravans traversed the land routes between India and Europe while cargo-laden ships sailed between India's southern coast and ports in southern Egypt. The wealth that flowed into India as the result of all this trade eventually formed the economic basis for a powerful new kingdom, the Gupta Empire.

Founded in the fourth century A.D., the Gupta Empire eventually expanded, as the result of military action, to encompass most of northern India. Despite the military nature of the regime, the third Gupta king, Chandragupta II, was a benevolent ruler. He was a Hindu king who fully tolerated and supported the many Buddhists who lived in India. During these prosperous and mostly peaceful times, he encouraged the development of art, science, architecture, and philosophy. Chandragupta II was so successful in this that the Gupta period (A.D. 320–540) is often called the classical age of India. Masterpieces of literature and poetry were written in Sanskrit, the language of the time that forms the basis of Hindi and other modern Indian languages. Many great Hindu temples and Buddhist monasteries were built, including the twenty-nine remarkable hand-carved temple-caves at Ajanta in central India. Several excellent Indian universities attracted students from all over Asia. Indian scientists of the time knew that the world was round and that it rotated about its axis, facts that were not accepted in Europe for almost another thousand years. At the time, India was clearly the most civilized country on earth.

The glory of the Gupta period was to last only a little more than two hundred years. In the middle of the fifth century A.D., the Gupta Dynasty was brought down by a series of invasions by Huns, warrior tribes from central Asia. The Huns also interrupted the essential trade routes across Asia and blocked the flow of goods that had made the Gupta period so prosperous. The subcontinent once again became a collection of feuding small Hindu kingdoms, and India entered its own Dark Ages, coinciding with the same dismal period in Europe.

The Ajanta temples, carved from solid rock, are a lasting monument to the spiritual devotion of the Guptas.

THE INVENTION OF ZERO AND THE DECIMAL SYSTEM

The formal study of mathematics, sponsored by monasteries, temples, and guilds, became more advanced in India than anywhere else in the world during the Gupta period. Mathematicians created a system for writing numbers that was later adopted by Arab scholars and introduced to Europe as Arabic numerals. A fifth-century Indian mathematician and astronomer named Aryabhatta explained how to calculate the occurrence of eclipses and discovered the concepts of zero and decimals centuries ahead of the Europeans. The great Indian scientist V. S. Ramachandran named Aryabhatta's innovations "the most important inventions of the last two millennia. . . . Until his time, if you wanted to multiply two numbers, using the Roman system, it took an hour and an entire wall."

SOUTH INDIAN HISTORY

Since ancient times, south India, being far from the mountain passes where invaders entered the subcontinent from central Asia, enjoyed greater peace and stability than north India. The main language in the south was and still is Tamil, an ancient Dravidian language that scholars consider the oldest living language in the world. Of the ancient Tamil dynasties, the two known as the Pallara (eighth to ninth century) and the Chola (ninth to tenth century) united south India. Both dynasties had strong seafaring traditions and left lasting cultural and architectural influences on other south Asian civilizations in addition to south India.

ISLAM COMES TO THE SUBCONTINENT

In the meantime a new religion, Islam, had arisen in the west of the Arabian Peninsula. Muslims, as adherents to Islam are called, believe fervently in one god and that they should wage holy war if necessary to spread the faith among non-Muslims. The first Muslim raider to reach the Indian subcontinent was the Turkish sultan Mahmud, who led his army into the Punjab on plundering raids. He was not interested in conquering India, and after a raid he returned to his fortress in Ghazni (in the center of present-day Afghanistan). These exploratory raids established the Khyber Pass as the best route into the subcontinent and demonstrated that the defenses of India were vulnerable.

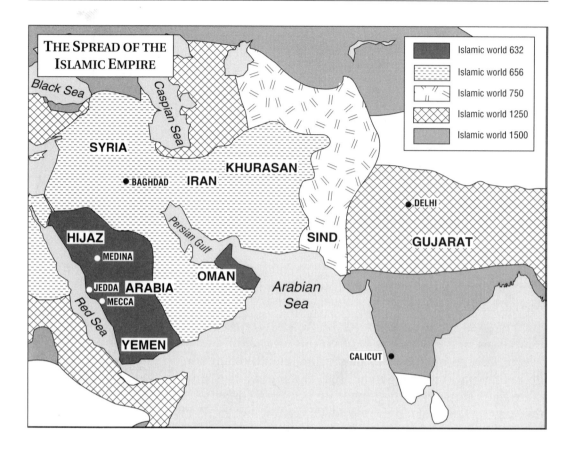

THE SPREAD OF THE ISLAMIC EMPIRE

■	Islamic world 632
	Islamic world 656
	Islamic world 750
	Islamic world 1250
	Islamic world 1500

Following the same route through the Khyber Pass that Mahmud of Ghazni had used, the first Arab Muslim army reached the province of Sind (in present-day Pakistan) in 644. By 711, Muslims had conquered Sind and established deep Islamic roots there. The Arab warriors won converts by force, but the Islamic faith also appealed to low-caste and outcaste Hindus, so Muslims gradually became an increasingly important part of the Indian cultural mosaic.

Islam expanded into India at an uneven pace for the next five hundred years. By the thirteenth century, Muslim forces had established a command center at Delhi from which they conquered the Gangetic Plain and brought the entire northern half of India under their control. The Sultanate of Delhi, as the first established Muslim government in India is known, became the first real stabilizing force in India since the Gupta Empire. Eventually, five separate dynasties controlled the sultanate, each gaining power by violent overthrow of its predecessor. Throughout these changes, the sultanate remained strong enough to resist attacks by new Mongolian invaders from central Asia—with one exception.

At the time of the sultanate, Genghis Khan and other Mongols were wreaking havoc throughout much of Asia and eastern Europe. One of the fiercest Mongol warlords was Timur the Lame (also called Tamerlane). Timur succeeded in overrunning Delhi in 1398, but after sacking the capital, he and his army left northern India, to the relief of the sultanate.

While the Mongols stayed away for most of the next two hundred years, the Muslim sultanate was embroiled in frequent skirmishes with a fierce Hindu dynasty of warriors, the Rajputs. The Rajput resistance to the Muslim invaders contributed greatly to the eventual weakening of the sultanate. By the early sixteenth century, northern India had again disintegrated into a number of small states busily using up their resources in constant fighting with each other. This opened the door for two new waves of invaders, one from the steppes of Asia and the other from Europe. The first to arrive were the Moguls, who followed the northwestern line of attack pioneered by the Arabs and used most recently by the Mongol Timur.

The powerful conqueror Babur was India's first Mogul emperor.

THE MOGUL ERA

Like the Mongols to whom they were closely related, the Moguls came from central Asia and were great warriors. Unlike the Mongol Timur, however, the Moguls did not come to India simply to pillage and return home with the spoils. They came to conquer and rule, and in the process they changed Indian society and culture forever.

India's first Mogul emperor was Babur. Babur grew up in what is now southern Russia and became a boy king in his homeland when his father died in 1494. During the next twenty years, his skills as a warrior grew as he fought Turks, Persians, Afghans, and other Moguls, but he was eventually defeated and lost control of his kingdom in Russia. In possession of an army but no kingdom, he then turned his attention to the south. He took his army through the Khyber

Pass and into India, where he met with much greater success. He invaded India from Afghanistan five times in seven years. With ferocity and cunning, backed by superior cavalry and artillery, in 1526 he finally subdued what remained of the Sultanate of Delhi, and by 1529 most of the rest of northern India was also under his control.

After his death in 1530, Babur was followed by a succession of Mogul rulers, but Babur's grandson Akbar was by far the most influential. Akbar (1556–1605) came to the throne when he was only fourteen years old, but with the guidance of wise ministers he was able to claim complete and effective control of his empire while still a teenager.

The ruler Akbar of the Mogul Empire is pictured here with an officer of the Islam state. Akbar brought peace and prosperity to India by uniting the region's Muslims and Hindus.

Even though India's new rulers were Muslim, the vast majority of people living in the Mogul Empire were still Hindus. Many of them, particularly the Rajputs, were well armed and openly rebellious against the new regime. During Babur's reign, the Moguls had been under constant attack from the fierce Rajput warriors. When Akbar became emperor, at first he also fought the Rajputs. Then, recognizing that neither the Mongols nor the Moguls had been able to defeat the Rajputs in battle, he changed his approach. Part of his new thinking may have been because he fell in love with a Rajput princess and married her. He discarded most of the strict Mogul regime's Muslim laws that treated Hindus as second-class citizens. He declared Islam no longer the state religion, as it had been during Babur's reign. For the first time since Muslims had come to power in India, members of all religions were treated equally. Akbar further united India by placing strong Rajput leaders in important government positions. He also encouraged architecture, painting, music, and dance forms that combined Hindu and Muslim traditions.

Under Akbar's tolerant and wise leadership, India entered a period of unprecedented peace and prosperity, becoming one of the richest and most powerful nations in the world.

THE TAJ MAHAL, A MONUMENT TO LOVE

The magnificent Taj Mahal, known as the eighth wonder of the world, was built under Shah Jahan's direction. This was his memorial to his favorite wife, Mumtaz Mahal, who died in childbirth in 1631. Built of white marble and inlaid with semi-precious stones, it is considered by many people to be the most beautifully proportioned building in existence.

The Taj Mahal is located along the Yamuna River in the Mogul capital city of Agra, near Delhi. It was designed by a team of architects from India, Persia, and central Asia, and more than twenty thousand workers were employed in its construction. The entire complex took twenty-two years to complete. On either side of the Taj Mahal are two symmetrically identical red sandstone buildings not usually seen in photographs. One is a mosque and the other is its mirror image, built solely for the beauty of balance. The main dome of the Taj Mahal is so large and perfectly constructed that a sound made under its center can echo for up to twelve seconds. The tombs of Shah Jahan and his Mumtaz Mahal are located side by side in a vault below this dome.

The Taj Mahal was not always as appreciated as it is today. The premises were neglected after Aurangzeb jailed Shah Jahan, and the buildings began to decay during the Raj. The British made plans to dismantle the entire edifice and ship the pieces of pearly white marble to England. The only thing that prevented this from taking place was the lack of buyers at the price needed to make a healthy profit.

Eleanor Roosevelt summed up the majesty of the Taj Mahal when she wrote in 1953, "The white marble of the Taj symbolizes the purity of real love; and somehow love and beauty seem close together in this creation. . . . As long as I live I shall carry in my mind the beauty of the Taj, and at last I know why my father felt it was the one unforgettable thing he had seen in India."

The majestic Taj Mahal is famous for its architectural quality and unmatched beauty.

European countries became eager to establish friendly relations with Mogul India in order to share in its fabulous wealth through trade.

Akbar was succeeded by his son, Jahangir (1605–1627). Jahangir led an unsuccessful rebellion against his father, and as a result he was kept under house arrest until his pardon a few months before Akbar's death. But when Jahangir became emperor, he decided to follow in his father's footsteps and ruled with tolerance and wisdom. He became the first Mogul emperor to elevate his wife, Nur Jahan, to an influential position with considerable power in the kingdom. Nur Jahan helped to establish a precedent in India that made it acceptable for women to hold political power.

Jahangir's son, Shah Jahan (1628–1658), began a shift back to the strict Muslim ways, and he made Islam the state religion once again. He ordered many Hindu temples destroyed while building new mosques and forts, acts which alienated the Rajputs. As Shah Jahan aged, he began making more and more extravagant expenditures—including the building of the Taj Mahal and otherwise draining the empire's resources—which further increased discontent within the country. Disgusted with what they considered to be a great waste of funds, Shah Jahan's sons overthrew him and put their father in prison until his death.

One of Shah Jahan's sons, Aurangzeb (1658–1707), became the next Mogul ruler. Aurangzeb was a severe and humorless man and an even more devout Muslim than his father. He imposed extremely strict Islamic law on the empire, reinstated taxes that applied only to Hindus, and even persecuted Muslims from sects other than his own. His religious fanaticism led to numerous rebellions around the empire. He was so suspicious of everyone that he killed his own brothers and imprisoned his three sons and daughter because he believed they were plotting a rebellion.

The next Mogul leaders after Aurangzeb were weak. All around northern India, revolutions led by Rajput, Maratha, and other Hindu chieftains continually chipped away at the unity of the subcontinent until the glory of the Mogul Empire slipped away, even as a new wave of foreigners were invading the subcontinent.

FROM BRITISH COLONY TO THE WORLD'S LARGEST DEMOCRACY

Even as the Moguls were building their empire on the Indian subcontinent, an invasion of a different sort was already underway. Beginning in 1498 with the arrival by sea of the Portuguese explorer Vasco da Gama, emissaries from several European countries began establishing trading centers along the coasts of India. For a few years it seemed there might be enough trade to satisfy all the traders from Portugal, France, Holland, and England, but competition for Indian markets grew rapidly. Furthermore, a long series of wars in Europe had almost depleted the treasuries of many countries, so it was inevitable that competition for Indian riches would turn into violent conflicts. By 1700, the Europeans were fighting sea and land battles to gain control of access to Indian spices, fabrics, pearls, and other valuable commodities. Because of these battles, troops and warships were stationed at trading posts from the start. Eventually these military forces were turned against the Indians themselves.

In the struggles for control of trade with India, the various European powers acquired different Indian allies and often fought with armies composed of both Indians and Europeans. The British, represented by the British East India Company, succeeded in gaining the favor of the Mogul rulers and acquired formal status as the Mogul Empire's chief trading partner in return for providing military assistance. While the British fought enemies of the Moguls as well as the remaining European powers on the subcontinent, the Moguls, who by this point were losing their grip on the empire, authorized English representatives to begin collecting taxes for them. Great Britain saw the opportunity to become the dominant European power in India and seized it.

The British campaign in India attained its greatest successes under a brilliant commander named Robert Clive, a thirty-two-year-old former clerk of the British East India Company. His most remarkable victory was in 1757 at the Battle of Plassey (in the northeastern province of Bengal) against a larger but less disciplined French-backed Mogul force. After Plassey, the British East India Company took full control of Bengal, which gave England a solid base from which to expand its influence into other parts of India.

The Battle of Plassey marked the beginning of British rule in India. The British East India Company continued to expand its sphere of economic control even as British troops

THE PORTUGUESE—FIRST AND LAST EUROPEAN COLONISTS IN INDIA

The British ruled India for almost two hundred years, but they were not the first Europeans to enter India and they were not the last to leave. Both these honors go to the Portuguese.

While Christopher Columbus was looking for India in the Caribbean Sea, the Portuguese admiral Vasco da Gama was pioneering a sea route around Africa and across the Indian Ocean. Like Columbus, his exploration fleet consisted of three armed vessels. In 1498 he became the first European to reach India by sea when his tiny fleet anchored off the Malabar Coast. The spices he carried back to Portugal the following year earned enough profit to pay for his entire fleet and all the expenses of the journey thirty times over.

In 1510 the Portuguese established a fortified trading post in Goa on India's west coast. From there, they controlled the lucrative spice trade for most of the sixteenth century. Portugal eventually colonized and annexed Goa, and the Portuguese continued to control Goa until the Republic of India forced them out in 1961, fourteen years after the British left India.

The explorer Vasco da Gama was the first European to sail to India's coast.

continued military actions against the rulers of various Indian provinces who resisted doing business with the British. Back in England, there was considerable support for this aggression. An influential segment of the British population felt a moral superiority to what they considered to be the "uncivilized" people of the world. In India—that vast land of non-Christians, tribal populations, peasants, village dwellers, Dravidians, and Aryans—Victorian England found ample reasons to spread "civilization" and avoid chaos by exercising military control.

At first the British did not seek to rule India directly but instead developed a policy of allowing local rulers to stay in office while forcing them to pay "fees" to the representatives of the British East India Company for military protection. Led by Clive, individual officers of the company enriched themselves by demanding huge amounts of money from Indian rulers and carrying out all manner of unfair trade practices. Word of their excessive greed spread back to England, and the degree of looting and corruption committed by the British East India Company began to raise a demand among the British populace that Parliament put a halt to these excesses. Even though much of the fortune being made in India helped to finance the industrial revolution taking place in England, the call for reform, restraint, and sharing of the profits became too strong to ignore.

Lord Robert Clive's success at the Battle of Plassey led to British control of Bengal.

Finally, in 1784, the "Indian situation" had become such a large economic and political issue in Great Britain that the British prime minister, William Pitt, introduced a bill to reform and control the actions of the East India Company. The India Act, as it was called, was passed that same year. It placed the actions of the East India Company under the direct control of the government and led to huge changes in the nature of Britain's presence in India.

The man sent to direct these changes was Lord Cornwallis, fresh from losing to the American revolutionaries. He completely restructured the way British merchants operated in India, removed most of the opportunities for corruption, and streamlined the administration of the East India Company. In doing so, he established the basis for the reputable Indian Civil Service (ICS). The ICS was staffed with talented young Englishmen. Indian nationals were eventually employed by the ICS, but not under Lord Cornwallis. He had a deep distrust for Indians and refused to allow them to work in the East India Company, saying, "Every native of Hindustan I verily believe is corrupt."[3]

By 1818, the last armed resistance to British control was put down and the cleaned-up East India Company became the undisputed master of India. A diplomatic settlement made that year formally installed British rule in India. This settlement would remain in force with only minor changes until India achieved independence from England in 1947.

Great Britain had accomplished an amazing feat in turning India into a British colony. This accomplishment was made possible as much by the divisiveness of Indian society at the time as it was by the superior technology, tactics, and discipline of the British military. This was the first time that a relatively small European country had been able to subjugate an entire nation containing a unique civilization. How this came to be and how Great Britain maintained dominance over the subcontinent for almost two hundred years remains a source of fascination to this day.

Britain's Lord Cornwallis, sent to India to end corruption, founded the Indian Civil Service.

INDIA UNDER BRITISH RULE

Under the system begun by Lord Cornwallis, Great Britain governed India through the East India Company and the ICS. All significant positions of power were held by British citizens while most other positions, particularly those requiring direct contact with average Indian citizens, were held by Indians, who were paid generous salaries to discourage corruption. The British administrators of India also established a surprisingly fair judicial system that had, at least initially, judges who were all citizens of Great Britain. British directors set up and supervised an efficient tax collection system, and all top officials in the police force were British officers. The complex system designed to maintain British control of a

large number of Indian government officials left an unfortu-
nate legacy that survived to modern times—a government
burdened with a large, very slow, and exceedingly complex
bureaucracy.

Despite all of these changes, the day-to-day governing of
British India was conducted mostly by Indians. Furthermore,
the British system made every effort to preserve the traditional local leadership structure of India's villages, where
most of the country's population lived. On the other hand,
the British made English the language of government and
power, and so many Indians learned English that it continues to be one of the country's primary languages. Many other
Western ideas that were new to India were gradually ab-
sorbed into the Indian culture during British rule, including
equal treatment for all people under the law, ownership of
property, and English education standards.

THE SEPOY MUTINY

In 1857, less than a half century after Britain had taken firm
control of India, the latest rulers of the subcontinent suffered
their first serious setback. A series of uprisings throughout
the Ganges Valley and parts of central India resulted in a full-
scale war that lasted almost two years. The uprisings are

THE THUGS OF INDIA

No one wants to meet up with a thug in some
dark alley, but to meet an Indian Thug back in the eighteenth
century would have been even worse. The Thugs (from a
Hindi word meaning thief) were an organization of murderers
and thieves who specialized in strangling travelers in India.
The reason they strangled their victims was to preserve the
blood so it could be used as an offering to Kali, the Hindu goddess of destruction.

In 1800 it was estimated that there were about ten thousand Thugs in India. The predatory system called Thugee had
been in existence for at least six centuries, and during that
time Thugs were responsible for an estimated half-million
murders. Finally in 1833, the British launched a campaign that
resulted in the capture of thirty-two hundred of the cult's
members. Several hundred Thugs were hanged, which finally
ended their reign of terror.

called the Sepoy Mutiny (or Sepoy Rebellion) by the British, a deliberate understatement, and the Great War of Independence by Indian nationalists, a deliberate exaggeration.

The causes of these violent and bloody uprisings remain hard to unravel. The dismissal of local rulers, inefficient and unpopular as they might have been, proved to be a flashpoint in certain areas, but the spark that ignited revolt was the grease on British-issued bullets. A rumor, quite possibly true, leaked out that a new type of bullet issued to the sepoys, as Indian troops under British command were called, was greased with pig fat. At the same time, a similar rumor spread that the bullets were actually greased with cow fat. Pigs are unclean to Muslims and cows are holy to Hindus, and the sepoys were almost all Hindu or Muslim. The British were slow to deny these rumors and even slower in taking steps to prove either that they were incorrect or that changes had been made. The result was a loosely coordinated mutiny of the sepoy battalions of the Bengal Army of northern India. Of seventy-four sepoy battalions, seven remained loyal, twenty were quickly disarmed, and forty-seven began attacking British soldiers, houses, offices, and businesses. The

The bloody battles of the Sepoy Rebellion exemplified the dissension between the Indians and their British rulers.

THE REBEL QUEEN

When the Rana (king) of the north Indian province of Jhansi died, the British quickly claimed control of his kingdom on the weak excuse that he had no children to inherit it. His wife, Lakshmi Bai, the Rani of Jhansi, disagreed violently. When the Sepoy mutiny started a few years later, she joined the rebel cause. Dressed in men's clothing, she led the Jhansi army into battle. Numerous sepoys from neighboring regions joined her to swell the ranks of her army. Lakshmi Bai became an important leader of the Indian revolt, determined to rid India of the humiliating British domination. Her army captured the city of Gwalior and for a while resisted superior British forces. She was shot and killed in battle, and the Indians lost Gwalior and the rebellion. The Rani of Jhansi became one of the most famous symbols of India's struggle for independence.

rebellion broke out in the city of Meerut and soon spread across most of northern India. There were terrible massacres and cruel reprisals on both sides as the revolt continued to spread. It took British troops, aided by Indian Sikhs and Gurkas loyal to the British, more than a year to completely quell the rebellion. Peace was hindered by British cries for vengeance, and thousands of Indians were killed after short trials or no trials at all.

THE BRITISH RAJ

After the Sepoy Mutiny, Great Britain completely reorganized the armed forces all over the subcontinent, increased the percentage of British soldiers in the ranks, prohibited Indians from becoming officers, and allowed only British citizens to handle artillery. The British Parliament abolished the East India Company's rule and established direct rule of India under a British viceroy—the British ruler of India. The British cabinet was expanded to include a secretary of state for India who was responsible to Parliament. Then Queen Victoria was proclaimed "Empress of India," and British India became known as the "Raj," the Hindi word for kingdom. As a result, England also felt a greater sense of responsibility toward India and built many roads, railways, harbors, and a telegraph system under the direction of the highly efficient, British-run, Indian-manned ICS.

Probably the deepest impact of the war between the British and the sepoys, however, was the mountain of distrust that came to separate the white-skinned British rulers and their darker-skinned Indian subjects. Indians were now filled with fear of the British, but they also had given birth to an irrevocable hope of eventual independence from their European overlords.

The Raj became a highly efficient organization that blended European ideas with the diverse values, races, and peoples of the Indian subcontinent. Under this novel mixture of influences, the Indian society and economy underwent a period of unprecedented change to a degree that has never been duplicated before or since in the East or the West.

THE RISE OF INDIAN NATIONALISM

The racial attitudes of the British, attitudes that denied social equality to even Western-educated Indians, was a constant insult to Indians. Added to this humiliation was a British scheme to turn India into a source of raw materials for European industrialization. Demands among Indians for national autonomy became louder, and in 1885 the Indian

LIFE AS A SAHIB IN THE TIME OF THE RAJ

During the Raj, most British citizens living in India led lives of great luxury, with Indian servants waiting on them hand and foot. For the most part, the Europeans remained separate from the Indians. They lived in "cantonments" that were physically and culturally distant from the towns and bazaars, and they socialized in whites-only clubs. The only "natives," as the British began calling the Indians, in the British areas were the servants, without whom the luxurious lifestyle of the sahibs (white men) and memsahibs (white women) would have been impossible. Social life in the cantonments centered around the clubs, where the attitude of racial superiority toward Indians continued to thrive. Many Englishmen living in the cantonments held tight to the conviction that whites had a moral obligation to bring European culture to what they viewed as the heathen natives of India. This conviction, described as "the white man's burden" by the British writer Rudyard Kipling, was widespread in the British cantonments of India even as it was becoming unacceptable back in England.

National Congress was founded to represent the various movements for independence that were appearing all over the country.

By 1900, opposition to British rule began to take on a new urgency. The Indian National Congress, which was to become the Congress Party, began to push for self-rule. Eventually, the British agreed to work toward Indian independence as they had in Canada and Australia. When World War I engulfed Europe, Britain postponed action on these plans. Then, in the midst of increasingly harsh treatment of Indian nationalists and their supporters, deteriorating economic conditions, continuing racial attitudes, and a lack of concrete steps toward giving India its independence, a great social, spiritual, and political leader emerged.

GANDHI

In 1915, a young English-educated Indian attorney named Mohandas Karamchand Gandhi (1869–1948) returned to his homeland from South Africa, where he had been working on behalf of immigrant Indians who were suffering under extreme discrimination. Within a few years of his return to India, he became leader of the Congress Party and formed it into a disciplined, well-funded organization focused on achieving self-government for India.

With the memory of the bloody Indo-British violence of the Sepoy Mutiny still in the minds of Indians everywhere, Gandhi surprised many by calling for an entirely nonviolent response to the British inequities. He gradually raised the political awareness in the villages, where the vast majority of Indians lived, which gave the Congress Party the ability to mobilize huge numbers of supporters for independence.

In 1920, a British Army contingent opened fire on a large, unarmed crowd of Congress Party protesters at Jallianwallah Bagh near the Golden Temple in Amritsar. Approximately three hundred people were killed and twelve hundred wounded. This slaughter marked the starting point of a more intense opposition to the British rule that culminated in India's independence.

Following the Jallianwallah Bagh incident, Gandhi said, "Nonviolence and cowardice go ill together. I can imagine a fully armed man to be at heart a coward. Possession of arms implies an element of fear, if not cowardice. But true nonviolence is an impossibility without the possession of unadulterated fearlessness."[4]

So, despite episodes like the one at Jallianwallah Bagh, Gandhi continued his policy of passive, nonviolent resistance, fortifying it with propaganda, massive demonstrations, boycotts, noncooperation, and the gradual establishment of a parallel government that was ready to come forward when independence was granted. Gandhi stepped up the number and size of the demonstrations and led a massive march to the sea to collect sea salt as a protest against the Raj's hated tax on salt. He also successfully organized an ongoing boycott of imported British goods, especially textiles. The British jailed him repeatedly, but that just made the people rally to his cause in ever-greater numbers. With people back in England growing more sympathetic to India's struggle for independence, the Raj finally recognized the futility of trying to maintain control.

Mohandas Karamchand Gandhi is India's most celebrated leader because of his lifetime devotion to nonviolent protest.

The British, however, were not the only source of discord among Indians. The Muslims and Hindus argued passionately about how power in independent India was going to be divided, and violence between Indians of these two religions became a terrible problem. Gandhi, who never wavered in his unshakable belief in nonviolent protest and religious tolerance, would fast whenever fighting began. Because members of both religions held him in such high regard, the fighting would generally stop when the newspapers reported that "Gandhi-ji" was fasting.

During World War II, Britain made its last demands on India as its colony. It took stringent police measures to preserve the Raj against increasing Indian nationalism while England used India as both a supply and operations base. Many Indians served in the British military forces, and Indian industry was expanded to supply the war effort. While some parts of India benefited from the increased industrial production, war-related factors combined with lack of rain led to food shortages that resulted in 2 million deaths by starvation in Bengal between 1942 and 1944.

As World War II ended, the world knew that the era of colonialism was over. With independence looming, the first elections in India revealed as fact what many already feared—the country was split on purely religious grounds. The Muslim League, led by Mohammed Ali Jinnah, represented Muslims, and the Congress Party, led by Jawaharlal Nehru, represented Hindus. Gandhi, though nonpartisan and not wanting an official role in the government that was forming, remained a father figure for the Congress Party. A premonition of the terrible troubles that were about to descend on India came during one of Jinnah's speeches. To a crowd of angry and fearful Muslims he declared that the Muslim League would see India divided into a Muslim state and a Hindu state or they would destroy India.

Early in 1946, a British mission attempted to negotiate an agreement between the two sides that would allow them to live together in India as they had since Mogul times. The talks failed. India slid increasingly toward civil war, and in 1947 the

Religious differences between Hindus and Muslims have resulted in many deaths. Here, a Hindu lies dead in the streets of Calcutta after a riot.

Muslim League called for a "direct action" day that deterio-
rated into a slaughter of Hindus in Calcutta. The Hindus re-
sponded with deadly reprisals against the Muslims. As the
bloodshed continued, Gandhi went on another fast, starving
himself almost to death before the fighting finally stopped.

The new and last viceroy of British India, Lord Mountbatten, made a last ditch attempt to convince the rival factions
that a united India was a more sensible proposition than dividing it into two countries, but Jinnah and his Muslim
League continued to demand a separate country for Muslims. Reluctantly, Mountbatten made the decision to divide
India. In the end, only Gandhi stood firm against the division, preferring the possibility of a civil war to the terrible
events he was sure would occur if India was divided.

The problem was made worse by the fact that a neat division of India into two parts was impossible. Although some
areas were clearly Hindu and others clearly Muslim, the
main Muslim areas were on extreme opposite ends of the
subcontinent. Furthermore, many areas had evenly mixed
populations of both religions, and others had isolated populations of Muslims surrounded by Hindus.

The final division was as awkward a political solution as
ever devised. The new Muslim nation, Pakistan, had an eastern portion and a western portion divided by the vast bulk of
mostly Hindu India. The impossibility of dividing all the
Muslims from all the Hindus was illustrated by the fact that
even after the country was divided into East and West Pakistan for the Muslims and India for the Hindus, India was still
the third largest Muslim country in the world. Only Indonesia and Pakistan had larger populations of Muslims.

Once the awkward division was decided upon, Mountbatten moved quickly, announcing that India and Pakistan
would become independent nations within days. At mid-
night on August 14, 1947, the subcontinent became independent from British rule. Chopped up and on the brink of
its first war with Pakistan, India was finally independent.

For the next several months, the greatest exodus in human
history took place east and west across the subcontinent.
Trainloads of fleeing Muslims were held up and slaughtered
by Hindu and Sikh mobs while Hindus and Sikhs fleeing in
the other direction suffered the same fate at the hands of
Muslim mobs. In the province of Punjab alone, during the

Millions of Indians sought new homes after independence from Britain and the division of India in 1947.

first three months after independence more than 10 million people had changed sides and around a half million people had lost their lives.

Then on July 30, 1948, a Hindu extremist who was angry at Gandhi for urging fair treatment of Muslims and all other faiths shot and killed him. In the end, the man who had said, "Love is the subtlest force in the world,"[5] was killed by hatred.

Gandhi became known in his lifetime as the Mahatma (Great Soul), not only because of his role in leading India to independence but because his steadfast opposition to violence and his moral courage inspired people everywhere. Albert Einstein, for example, was moved to say of Gandhi, "Generations to come will scarce believe that such a one as this ever in flesh and blood walked upon this earth."[6] Martin Luther King Jr. was strongly influenced by Gandhi and incorporated Gandhi's nonviolent approach in the American civil rights movement.

A New Era

Jawaharlal Nehru, the first prime minister of free India, believed passionately that democracy presented the best means of holding India together and bringing the social and economic changes that would benefit the most people. Nehru was enormously popular and could have appointed himself king or even dictator, but instead he practiced his beliefs, including his faith in democratic government, an independent judiciary, and a free press. The standards he set became the accepted political standards for India, the largest democracy in the world.

During Nehru's time as prime minister (1947 until his death in 1964), the first Indian constitution became law and India became a true republic in 1950. In addition, sweeping social and economic reforms were begun, industrial production rose, and new health programs lowered the national mortality rate. On the other hand, agricultural growth failed to keep pace with population growth, and several wars and skirmishes with Pakistan and China occurred.

Two years after Nehru's death, his daughter, Indira Gandhi, was elected prime minister. She served three terms and gradually became a strong leader who made many enemies. During her first two terms as prime minister, India increased agricultural production and approached self-sufficiency in food production, exploded its first nuclear bomb (1974), and had another war with Pakistan. Mrs. Gandhi offended millions by forcing sterilization on many poor Indians. With a variety of other problems erupting around the country, and facing growing political opposition, she declared a state of emergency and abolished most civil liberties. She also had six hundred opponents thrown into prison without trial, and she instituted censorship of the press. Even though she relaxed the emergency provisions and released opposition members from jail before the next elections, she lost to Moraji Desai of the Janata Party in 1977.

In 1980, with the Janata Party in disarray, Indira Gandhi was reelected prime minister. Four years later, Sikh nation-

Prime Minister Jawaharlal Nehru brought democracy to India, and the country prospered as a republic.

alists demanding an autonomous Sikh state occupied several places of worship. Federal troops
stormed the Golden Temple in Amritsar, the
most holy center of the Sikh faith. Soon after
that incident, Mrs. Gandhi was assassinated by
two Sikh members of her personal team of
bodyguards.

In 1984, Mrs. Gandhi's son, Rajiv Gandhi, was
elected the next prime minister by an overwhelming majority, but his popularity faded as
policies he introduced failed. Then amidst alle-
gations of corruption in Rajiv Gandhi's government, V. P. Singh, the leader of the new Janata
Dal Party became prime minister in 1989.

During the next decade, the great old party of
India, the Congress, failed to hold a majority for
long. In fact, frequently shifting allegiances prevented any party from staying in power for
long, and the government was characterized by numerous
fragile and mostly short-lived coalitions. Violence resulting
from both political and social causes has plagued India's
election campaigns since Indira Gandhi's days, extending
even to her son, Rajiv Gandhi, who was assassinated in 1991
while campaigning for reelection.

*Indira Gandhi made
many enemies during
her tenure as prime
minister.*

4

Spiritual and Ethnic Diversity

India is home to about a sixth of the world's population, and within that billion or so people are members of almost every race and religion on earth. Indians speak more than a dozen different languages and many people, especially in the south, cannot understand Hindi, India's official language. Indians practice half a dozen religions, and each of those religions has numerous sects and subsects. There are literally dozens of political parties.

Inevitably such diversity creates deep and ancient social divisions, and yet with all these differences India remains the world's largest democracy. There are enormous problems in India; and, to many people, Indians and outsiders alike, it seems a miracle that this amazingly diverse country continues to function as a free society.

A Nation of Religions

India is officially a secular country because it does not recognize any specific religion in the constitution, but the spiritual life of India determines the nation's character to a degree unequaled in any Western country, perhaps to a degree unequaled in any other country in the world. Religion defines Indian society, and daily life in India, far more than in Western societies, is charged with religious meaning. Besides its importance in family and personal life, religion is also a major determinant of virtually all Indian political and social movements. This was reiterated by Gandhi: "I can say without the slightest hesitation, and in all humility, that those who say that religion has nothing to do with politics do not know what religion means."[7]

The subcontinent gave birth to two of the world's major religions, Hinduism and Buddhism. For several millennia India has been a land of religious diversity, and that remains true today. About 80 percent of India's people are Hindus, but the country is also home to over 100 million Muslims (only Indonesia and Pakistan have more people of the Islamic faith), 22 million Christians (more than the entire population of many European countries), 18 million Sikhs, 7.5 million Buddhists, 4 million Jains, and numerous members of many other faiths.

With all the religious tolerance that exists in India, there are also serious religious conflicts. In the villages where people still know each other as individuals, Hindus, Muslims, and Sikhs coexist relatively peacefully, but in the crowded cities it is often a different story. There, long-standing resentments lurk just below the surface and, too often, interreligious antagonisms explode into violence. In November of 1984, India experienced some of the worst religious violence since independence. For three terrible days following Indira Gandhi's assassination by her Sikh bodyguards, murderous Hindu mobs chanting "Blood for blood" controlled the streets of the nation's capital, and neither Delhi's officials nor the central government moved against them. At least twenty-seven hundred and perhaps as many as five thousand Sikh men and boys were killed before the riot ended.

Despite such conflicts, religion, even at the dawn of the twenty-first century, provides the foundation and much of the structure of Indian society.

HINDUISM

Hinduism is the oldest living faith in the world. Because of its absolutely central role in Indian life, it is essential to understand this religion in order to understand India.

Cars burn in New Delhi during the riots touched off by the assassination of Indira Gandhi.

It is more accurate to describe Hinduism as a way of life rather than a religion. Hinduism is less a single religious system than a spectrum of interwoven, loosely related traditions and spiritual activities that allow a person considerable choice in how to practice the faith. There is no totally exclusive set of beliefs that every Hindu must accept; instead there is a cluster of related questions every Hindu asks of life, deity, and self.

The word Hindu was originally a geographic designation derived from Sind, the Sanskrit name for the Indus River. Europeans, not resident Indians, gave the name "Hindu" to the religious practices known to orthodox practitioners as *Sanatana-Dharma* (Eternal Duty).

Though Hinduism's earliest roots are lost in prehistory, apparently it acquired its present-day Vedic traditions during the second millennium B.C. as nomadic Aryan-speaking in-

THE SACRED COWS

The fact that cows are sacred in India is well known, but many Westerners think this has something to do with the fact that many Hindus do not eat meat. Ideas of not harming animals, including killing them for food, are important to Hindus and others; but to a Hindu, the animal is a "holy cow" because of the notion of purity.

One of the primary ethical concerns of Hinduism is the purity of the soul that is needed to attain the supreme goal of Hinduism, which is release from the reincarnation cycle of births and deaths. This purity takes both spiritual and physical forms, and milk—white, clean, unspoiled milk—is one of the purest substances and used regularly in a number of Hindu rituals. The cow, the giver of milk, is therefore revered and protected throughout India because of its great purity and as the sacred embodiment of motherhood and fruitfulness.

A bull stands in a busy street of Ahmedabad. To Hindus, cows are sacred.

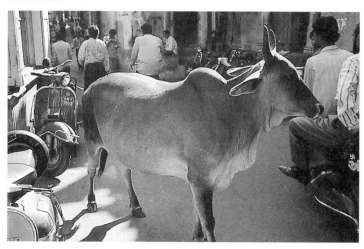

vaders mixed with the original Dravidian inhabitants of the Indus Valley region. Through the intervening centuries, the original Vedic tradition has been added to and modified by the epic stories and myths of different localities to form the highly diverse and complex system that is modern Hinduism.

Hinduism is so diverse that it can accommodate monotheism, polytheism, and atheism (belief in one god, many gods, and no god). What is more, Hinduism accommodates different views of and different rituals for the same deity. Hinduism can be all things to all people, and this forms the basis for the tolerance that typifies Indian life.

Hinduism is based on a large body of ancient Sanskrit literature known as the four Vedas and more recent writings. The Vedas, passed down orally from generation to generation, were not put into written form until between 1200 and 600 B.C. The oldest and most important Vedic text is the Rig-Veda, a collection of lyric verses describing the interventions of the gods in human affairs. The most philosophical part of the Vedas are the Upanishads, which speculate about the nature of the universe. There are also two other important Hindu religious works, the *Mahabharata* and the *Ramayana*. These two epic poems spell out Hinduism's moral foundations in stories that are so well told that they influence the most popular stories in Indian television and stage entertainment today. Since Hinduism is an evolving and flexible set of beliefs, more "recent" books and stories were added during the first twelve centuries A.D.

The original Vedic deities numbered thirty-three, but the major deities of modern Hinduism have so many manifestations and incarnations, each with a different appearance and name, that the number of gods is far greater. Everything begins with Brahman, the essence of all things, the impersonal soul of the universe. Brahman is unimaginable and cannot be portrayed, although the sound "om" is believed to represent this basic essence. Brahman appears only as the three principal deities of Hinduism, Brahma the Creator, Vishnu the Preserver, and Siva the Destroyer. Vishnu, the most popular of these three, is pictured as a deity with four arms and usually sleeping on his couch, awakening whenever evil threatens the world. It is believed that there are ten avatars, or incarnations, of Vishnu, nine past and one to come. The most beloved of these are Rama, Krishna, and

Buddha. Kali, the destroyer of worlds, is yet to come. One extremely popular deity is Siva's son Ganesha, the elephant-headed, fat and happy deity known as the remover of obstacles. Other frequently seen deities, both in temples and in homes, are Hanuman, the monkey god worshipped as the god of physical strength; beautiful Kama, revered as the goddess of love; Nandi, the great bull; Chandra, the moon god; and Naga, the cobra god.

Many Hindu villagers worship Vishnu, Siva, and any of the other gods as local need or custom dictates without any sense of one being more or less important than the others. At the more intellectual level, Hindus see the gods as mere parts of the Brahman, the godhead that is everywhere and in everything and everyone.

During their lives, Hindus must perform three types of duties, usually likened to paths. These are the intellectual path of mental discipline, the emotional path of love, and the selfless path of service. A devout Hindu will practice nonviolence, truth, and detachment while traveling these paths. Hindus believe in karma, the idea that actions in this life affect the next life.

Hindus view life as divided into four stages: the joyous innocence of childhood, the mental and physical discipline of student life, the devotion to family life, and the renunciation of material things in preparation for the final years. During the fourth stage, many Hindu men so completely withdraw from the material world that they become full-time holy men, or sadhus, and spend all their lives in meditation and religious service. Some become respected spiritual teachers known as gurus.

A statue of Siva as Nataraja, the cosmic dancer, stands at Mahabalipuram Temple.

ISLAM

Islam was imported into India by Muslim conquerors and Arab merchants. Its founder, Muhammad, was born in Mecca in present-day Saudi Arabia in the sixth century A.D. Muslims believe that divine revelations came to Muhammad directly

THE HINDU JUGGERNAUT

In English the word "juggernaut" refers to something that is so powerful and large with so much momentum that it is practically unstoppable. Most people would never guess that this word comes from the name of a Hindu god.

In parts of India, especially the east and south, Lord Jaggernatha, an avatar of Vishnu, is worshipped with a spectacular procession. Once a year a large statue of Jaggernatha is placed on an immense wagon-like device that weighs many thousands of pounds. Its wooden wheels are twice the height of a man. The wagon, which is called a "car," has no motor and is so large that in some cities an entire family of caretakers use it as their home. Moving the car with its statue of Jaggernatha through the streets requires the effort of hundreds of devotees pulling dozens of ropes. The route that Jaggernatha's car takes each year can be identified by the smashed corners of the buildings where the car turned too sharply.

from God and that these are collected in the sacred book called the Koran. Unlike Hinduism, Islam was complete at the moment it began and is not open to interpretation or change, at least theoretically.

Islam means submission to God. The five required duties of the Muslim are: reciting the creed that there is no god but God (in Arabic, Allah) and Muhammad is his prophet; praying in a prescribed manner five times a day while facing Mecca; fasting during the holy month of Ramadan; charitable giving; and making a pilgrimage or hajj to Mecca once during a lifetime.

A Muslim stands in a personal relationship to God, and so there is no clergy in orthodox Islam. Those who lead prayers or interpret Islamic law do so by virtue of their superior wisdom and scholarship, not because they have been ordained with special powers.

Even though Muhammad described only one way to worship Allah, the passing years have raised disputes on the exact meaning of Muhammad's teachings. As a result, there are now two major divisions among Muslims in India and the world over, divisions that sometimes have resulted in violent confrontations between Muslims. These two divisions of the Islamic faith are Shia and Sunni, and most Indian

Muslims praying at the Jami Masjid (Principal Mosque) in Delhi.

Muslims are Sunnis. A mystical offshoot of Sunnism, the Sufis, incorporate elements of Hinduism in their religious practices.

Even though Muslims account for only 14 percent of its population, India has more Muslims than all but two other countries in the world. It is not unusual in Muslim areas of India to see a bus at the side of the road at prayer time with the passengers and driver outside, shoes off, prayer rugs spread, in rows on their knees and praying. Muslims may pray anywhere, but whenever possible they pray in a mosque.

SIKHISM

Sikhism appeared in the fifteenth century A.D. in northern India. It incorporates influences from Muslim Moguls, Christian missionaries, and Hinduism. Today 2 percent of the Indian population are Sikhs with the majority living in Punjab.

The founder of Sikhism was Nanak Dev (1469–1539), the first of ten gurus of the Sikh community. Since Punjab is the

Sikh homeland, the fifth Sikh guru, Arjan Das, selected the Punjabi city of Amritsar as the site for the Golden Temple, which is the Sikhs' spiritual center and most holy *gurdwara* (place of worship). The first five Sikh gurus wrote the hymns and teachings of the Sikh faith and compiled them in the Sikh scriptures called the Guru Granth Sahib. These teachings show strong Islamic and Hindu influences, but they also reject the Hindu caste system and certain Islamic rituals like the five daily prayers and the pilgrimage to Mecca. Central to the Sikh faith is the doctrine of One God, called simply Ikk (meaning "One"). Sikhs believe that God can be known only through loving devotion.

Traditionally, Sikh men are raised to be warriors with fearless courage, an attribute indicated by the surname that all Sikhs possess, Singh, which means "lion." Most Sikh men also wear what are commonly referred to as the five Ks: *kes* (beard and uncut hair under a turban), *kangha* (a special comb), *kirpan* (a sword or knife), *kara* (a steel bracelet worn on the right wrist), and *kaccha* (a type of short pants worn as an undergarment).

When the subcontinent was divided into Pakistan and India in 1947, the partition cut the Sikh homeland in half. Most of the Sikhs on the Pakistani side fled into the part of the Punjab that had become Indian territory. Since the 1950s, many Sikhs have believed they should have an autonomous

Guards stand outside the Golden Temple, the most holy place of worship for the Sikhs.

state where they are the majority and Punjabi is the state language. In 1966 this demand was granted, but that was not enough for some who wanted an independent Sikh nation. Sikh terrorists repeatedly and violently confronted the Indian government, most disastrously in 1984 when federal troops invaded the Golden Temple and killed several hundred Sikhs.

Sikhs comprise one of the best-educated, most prosperous communities in India. Their capital of Chandigarh in Punjab is a well-planned, modern, and clean city. Sikhs are prominent in the military, civil, and police services, especially in northern India.

BUDDHISM

Buddhism was founded in the sixth century B.C. by a wealthy Indian prince, Siddhartha Gautama, who gave up all his earthly possessions and devoted himself to contemplation of the mysteries of life. He became known as the Buddha (Enlightened One) after achieving mystical enlightenment.

The Buddha's teachings are based on an understanding of the mystery of human existence that he gained from his lengthy meditations. The essence of these teachings is the Four Noble Truths. The first Noble Truth is that all life is sorrow and suffering. The second Noble Truth is that all sorrow comes from the desire for and attachment to people and objects that can be destroyed or lost. The third Noble Truth is that stopping desire will end sorrow. The fourth Noble Truth describes how to stop all desire by following a system of spiritual discipline that Buddhists call the Middle Way. Buddhists believe that the world as experienced by humans is an illusion and that it is necessary to endure a series of rebirths to escape the life of illusion and attain nirvana, a state of everlasting peace and total wisdom. Like the Hindus, Buddhists also believe in karma, the idea that actions in this life affect the next life.

As a new religion, Buddhism quickly gained popularity in India largely as a reaction to the Hinduism of the day, especially the caste system. After the founder's death, as in other religions a number of conflicting schools of thought concerning his teachings developed. Buddhism spread to Sri Lanka, Tibet, Southeast Asia, and East Asia, all areas where it is a major religion today. In India, however, Buddhism now accounts for only about 2 percent of the population. Furthermore, the Buddhism practiced in India today mixes Hindu practices and Buddhist doctrine, and Buddha is revered as the ninth incarnation of Vishnu. Even though Buddhism is no longer a leading religion in India, the Buddhist Wheel of Law (*dharma chakra*) is a national symbol that appears in the center of the country's flag.

JAINISM

Jainism is an ancient religion sharing much with Buddhism. Mahavira, a prince like Siddhartha who lived at the same time as the Buddha, founded Jainism as a Hindu reform religion. Mahavira, however, believed that it takes more drastic discipline to attain nirvana. Jains practice the Five Great Vows: nonviolence and noninjury to animals, truthfulness, avoidance of greed, avoidance of all sexual pleasure, and, like the Buddhists, nonattachment to the world of illusion. Jains do not eat meat, gamble, or drink alcohol, and as a result they have earned a high degree of respect.

Jains take the principle of noninjury to animals to great lengths. Many Jains wear masks to prevent accidentally harming insects by inhaling them, and Jain monks may be seen carefully sweeping small creatures from the path so that they will not be stepped upon.

Jains make up less than 1 percent of the Indian population, and they are concentrated on the west coast in the Mumbai (Bombay) area. Their small communities are economically successful because their religious practices have limited their work to banking, business, and other professions that are generally well paying.

CHRISTIANITY

About 22 million Indians (2.4 percent of the population) are Christians of different denominations. There have been Christian communities in India almost as long as in Europe. St. Thomas the Apostle is said to have visited Kerala on the southwest coast of India in 52 A.D. The Portuguese and English left

A Jain stands with a mask covering part of his face.

MOTHER TERESA

Frail, tiny, soft-spoken, always draped in the white sari with blue border that is the uniform of her Missionaries of Charity, Mother Teresa was the world's most famous symbol of compassion. Though she brought her kindness to many troubled places, her life's work was in the slums of India's Calcutta, one of the most desperately poor places on earth.

Born Agnes Gonxha Bojaxhiu in 1910 in Yugoslavia, she went to Ireland when she was eighteen to became a Catholic nun. In 1929 she was sent to Calcutta to teach, and there she dedicated her life to helping the poor. In 1950 she set up the international order of the Missionaries of Charity. Her courage and work on behalf of the poorest people in the world earned her the respect of national leaders and more than fifty international awards, including the Nobel Peace Prize in 1979.

The slums remain, but the woman known as the Saint of the Gutters is gone. Mother Teresa died September 5, 1997, at the age of 87.

Mother Teresa will be remembered for her hard work in helping the poor. She was admired and loved by people throughout the world.

large Christian communities in several parts of India, and Christian missionaries from different countries have been active in India for more than a century.

ZOROASTRIANISM

Zoroastrianism was the religion of pre-Islamic Persia (present day Iran) that was imported to India between the eighth and tenth centuries A.D. by refugees from Muslim oppression. Of India's approximately two hundred thousand modern Parsis (as practitioners of Zoroastrianism are called), most live in Bombay.

A Parsi views the universe as a battleground between good and evil, and believes in one Supreme God. The holy scripture of Zoroastrianism is the Zend-Avesta (usually shortened to Avesta) which declares fire, water, and earth to be sacred. Parsis also believe that these fundamental elements must be kept always pure, so in the Zoroastrian faith the dead are not buried, cremated, or placed in rivers or the sea. Instead Parsis put their dead on "towers of silence," where they are exposed to the vultures and other birds hovering constantly around the towers.

LANGUAGES

Outsiders have often asked how a country that cannot communicate with itself can remain a nation. Apparently in this land where there are fifteen constitutionally recognized languages and over sixteen hundred minor languages and dialects, Indians are also perplexed by this question. A 1997 survey in the national news magazine *India Today* found that Indians are eager to have a common language. Nevertheless, the only language that might be a contender for that honor, Hindi, is understood by less than a third of the Indians living in the central plateau (the Deccan) and the southern part of the country. The "language question," as it is called in countless discussions in the polylingual Indian press, is a sensitive political issue, and efforts to agree upon a single national

INDIA'S JEWS

One legend states that Jews first settled in India in the time of King Solomon when there was trade in teak wood, ivory, spices, and peacocks between the land of Israel and the Malabar Coast in the south of India, but most contemporary scholars are sure only that there were Jewish communities in Cochin on the coast of southern India by the twelfth century A.D.

Today there are approximately six thousand Jewish Indians. Although they are scattered around the country, there are still Jews in Cochin. The Cochin Jews consist of the so-called Black Jews (Malabris) who regard themselves as descendants of the original Jewish settlers, and the White Jews (Paradesim) who immigrated more recently from the Middle East and Europe.

Jews, like Christians, live outside India's caste system, although they have a strict code of their own. The country's Hindi majority exhibit a complete absence of discrimination toward the Jewish community. The Indian government has placed honor guards at the historic Cochin synagogue and even issued a postage stamp to commemorate the four hundredth anniversary of the building of the synagogue.

language have been unsuccessful. So for the foreseeable future, the language dilemma will continue, with hundreds of newspapers, other publications, and cable television channels keeping a polylingual society informed in a multitude of languages.

The constitution of India names Hindi as the country's official language, even though English is widely spoken (20 percent of the population speak it as their first language and a third more read and write it). For many educated Indians, English is their first language, and for a great many multilingual Indians, English is their second language.

In many cases, India's state boundaries were drawn not on geographical features like rivers but rather on linguistic lines. The names of many Indian states sound like the names of local languages, and in fact they are. Assamese, Bengali, Gujarati, Kashmiri, Tamil, Marathi, Punjabi, and Oriya are all languages with states named after them.

Although there are many languages in India, most of them evolved from one of two families of languages, Indo-Aryan and Dravidian. About three quarters of the population speak an Indo-Aryan language, a group of languages that are related to Indo-European, to which nearly all European languages belong. Sanskrit, one of the oldest languages in the world, is the original language of the Aryan invaders and all of the early Hindu religious scriptures. About a quarter of the people, mostly in the southern third of the country, speak languages based on ancient Dravidian. Both of these language families commonly borrow words and structures from one another as well as from English, Persian (Farsi), and Chinese.

ETHNIC DIVERSITY

Through the millennia, people from Central Asia, the Middle East, and Eastern Europe have contributed to India's ethnic mix. Today it is not possible to categorize Indians by their racial origins except in the broadest terms. In the north and northwest of the country, most people show Aryan characteristics: generally tall, dark haired, and fair skinned. The Rajputs of Rajasthan are considered to be direct descendants of the Huns of Central Asia. In the south of India more people have Dravidian characteristics: generally dark skinned and shorter. In the eastern part of the country, most people exhibit a blend of Mongoloid and Dravidian features.

A Hindu woman stands holding her baby. Hinduism is one of many religions practiced in India today.

How democracy can survive amidst the great spiritual and ethnic diversity of India is a source of wonder to many people. Perhaps these words, written more than two thousand years ago in one of India's ancient spiritual books, the Atharva Veda, best express the tolerant and cooperative spirit of the Indian people:

We are the birds of the same nest,
We may wear different skins,
We may speak different languages,
We may believe in different religions,
We may belong to different cultures,
Yet we share the same home.
Born on the same world,
Covered by the same skies,
Gazing at the same stars,
Breathing the same air,
We must learn to happily progress together
Or miserably perish together,
For man can live individually
But can survive only together.[8]

5

ART AND CULTURE

The art and culture of India incorporate many elements of religion, and this applies equally to dance, music, drama, poetry, literature, painting, sculpture, and crafts. Like religion, art is not seen as something separate from culture but as an everyday part of life. Furthermore, art is considered to be the language of the gods, and the goal of this language is to express the *rasas,* the nine feelings of life: happiness, anger, disgust, fear, sorrow, courage, compassion, wonder, and serenity.

THE VISUAL ARTS

A visitor to India quickly notices the great number of artistic legacies from the past. Indian architecture is like a great collage of different art forms, including design, sculpture, painting, and, in the case of the Taj Mahal, jewelry. It seems that almost every cliff or exposed rock has had at least one sculpture carved into it during the last two or three thousand years. India's rock sculptures range in size from small statuettes crudely chopped into the stone to entire temple complexes carved by expert craftsmen from solid rock on a scale that dwarfs Mount Rushmore.

Many Hindu temples seem to have as their primary goal the depiction of every event, deity, and person described in all the Vedas and religious epics. Painted figures and scenes cover every bit of space on south India's huge temples. The pillars and walls of Khajuraho's jewel-box-like temples are adorned with intricate and lifelike sculptures of heroes and heroines doing *everything* heroes and heroines are ever likely to do.

Over a period of a thousand years, Buddhist, Hindu, and Jain monks carved more than sixty full-sized temples from solid rock at Ajanta and Ellora in central India. These elaborate cave temples have massive and ornate pillars, huge statues, and detailed embellishments—all carved in place from solid rock. The most famous, the Kailasa temple at Ellora, is the largest sculpture cut from a single rock in the world. It took eight hundred workers a century and a half to complete it. Kailasa represents the mountain abode of Siva, complete with dozens of full-size elephants. Another Ellora temple features the shape of a flying chariot amidst the goddess Durga slaying a terrible demon in a flurry of flailing arms and weapons, all chiseled from solid rock. Other caves have two levels with wide staircases for access. Even the ceilings are carved in many of the caves, and in one the ceiling has been cut into an exquisite lotus blossom with a demoness sitting on a lion under a mango tree.

Indians have built many temples to honor their religious deities. This temple, dedicated to the deity Siva, was built during the Chandela dynasty.

Northern India possesses many excellent examples of inspired architecture from the Mogul era. The Islamic faith forbids sculpture depicting the human form, so mosques and other Muslim structures are lavishly decorated with verses from the Koran, geometric patterns, and flowers, often using semiprecious stones inlaid into the walls to make the building resemble a large piece of jewelry. All over Delhi, Mogul monuments, forts, mosques, and tombs are reminders that the city was once the center of the most prosperous country on earth.

THE TIGER AND THE CAVES

Because of an elusive tiger, the lost cave temples of Ajanta were rediscovered. In 1819, a group of British officers were tracking a large tiger when they found themselves in a gorge in the thickly wooded Sahyadri Hills of west-central India. Then one of the officers noticed what appeared to be a large cave, and after crossing a river to investigate, the group forgot all about the tiger.

By chance they had found a site lost for centuries, a series of thirty caves cut into the hills by monks between 200 B.C. and A.D. 650. The caves, which served as residences, temples, and schools, were entirely hand carved into the solid rock cliffs. The sculptures that adorn almost every surface of the caves include not only deities but dancing dwarfs playing musical instruments and beautiful women with every detail of their clothing shown. In some cases, the walls are covered with remarkable paintings that are still visible.

Walking through the caves today, visitors can feel the drama of those monks toiling for centuries to turn mountain faces into works of art, working with only natural light, the percussion of their hammers and chisels echoing in the gorge.

The cave temples of Ajanta, in Maharashta, were rediscovered in the nineteenth century after being "lost" for hundreds of years.

The British also contributed much to India's architectural heritage. Especially during the Raj they built elegant government buildings and monuments in all the major cities, most of which are still in use today. In New Delhi, for example, the former palace of the British viceroy is now the residence of the president of India. Many of the universities, churches, and libraries in the cities, with their soaring roofs and detailed decoration, look like they are straight out of Victorian England.

Painting in India also attained remarkable levels of refinement under the sponsorship of the royal courts of the Moguls. Mogul manuscripts illuminated with brilliant, Persian-inspired miniature paintings are world famous. Painting in modern India is, if less royal, just as inspired. A walk through a residential neighborhood in any Indian village or town will reveal countless examples of the way art is entwined with life and religion. Brightly colored religious folk art is everywhere, on the inside and outside walls of houses, in chalk on the ground before the front door, and even in inked patterns on women's palms.

Hand painting with henna is common among women in India.

No discussion of India's visual arts would be complete without mentioning Indian movies. For decades the Indian film industry has produced many more movies each year than Hollywood. Indian theaters are huge air conditioned buildings with special sections for families and provisions for eating entire meals during the movie. Indian popular movies are almost always at least three hours long and provide an escape from both the heat and the drudgery of daily life. Most films are simple love stories that always have big dancing and singing scenes with lavish costumes, glamorous stars who sing popular ballads, bad villains, silly sidekicks, guest appearances by various deities, and never any on-screen kissing. Not all Indian movies are so formulaic, however. The films of Satyajit Ray deal with the extraordinary lives of poor people and face issues of social change with honesty and compassion. Several of Ray's films have received critical acclaim in Western countries, including an Academy Award.

Until the late 1980s, India had only a handful of television stations, but with the advent of cable and the launch of several

Film posters cover buildings in Calcutta. The film industry thrives in India and movie production here is more extensive than in Hollywood.

Indian communications satellites, even in the villages this electronic "visual art" is replacing traditional modes of entertainment. Unfiltered Western programming with dubbed local languages now reaches all of India. MTV, BBC, and CNN compete with commercial Indian networks, and American soap operas and series like *Baywatch* are as popular as Indian-made programming.

DANCE AND DRAMA

Except for the relatively recent introduction of some Western styles, most Indian music and dance forms were developed at least five hundred years ago and therefore are called classical. It is said that even forms dating from the relatively recent Mogul era are based on the poetry of the ancient Vedas. For example, according to tradition, the seven-note scale of Mogul court music (Western music relies on an eight-note scale) was originally formulated by the Hindu god Siva, the King of Dancers. Most of the various expressive hand positions that are characteristic of classical Indian dance as well as dancers' attire, ornaments, and the stage can be recognized in descriptions in the Vedas.

Dance in India has seeped into the country's poetry, sculpture, architecture, literature, music, and theater. The oldest archeological find in India, dated around 6000 B.C., is a statuette of a dancing girl in a pose that is used by classical dancers today. All Indian classical dance forms are structured around the nine *rasas* and the idea that life is a balance between opposites. A frequent and popular theme is romantic love between two gods or between a god and a mortal.

Most contemporary styles of classical dances developed during the period between A.D. 1300 and 1400. The most celebrated art form in the southern Indian state of Tamil Nadu is the dynamic and earthy dance style called Bharata Natyam. This classical dance is extremely demanding of the dancers and requires years of total dedication and practice to master. Most Bharata Natyam dancers are women and, like the sculptures from which they take their positions, they always dance bent-kneed and use a wide variety of hand gestures to convey moods and expressions.

It often surprises Westerners how much romance and religion are mingled in India, and in fact the Hindu faith views all aspects of life as sacred, and that certainly includes romantic

Because it takes years to learn and perfect their art, Bharata Natyam dancers are considered among the most dedicated dancers in India.

love. Bharata Natyam dance is therefore religious and romantic, based as it is on love stories of the gods. The tempo is slow and each phase of the performance is distilled into a specific mood of love. Likewise, the northern Indian classical dance called Kathak, though performed straight-legged and with more emphasis on footwork than hand gestures, is also based upon romantic stories from religious scriptures.

In addition to the classical dances, India is rich in folk dances. Each area of the country has its own folk dances, including martial forms, seasonal and agricultural celebrations, religious rituals or instruction, and even dances that perform magic, but they all share a common heritage of religious stories and symbols.

Classical Indian drama is not a separate artistic endeavor like the Western style of theater based on narrative plays. Instead Indian theater combines storytelling, dance, and music. The clearest example of this is Kathakali, the rich and flourishing tradition of dance-drama centered in the beautiful tropical state of Kerala in southern India. When the evening falls and the drums beckon the people to the courtyard of the local temple, it is time for the magnificent spectacle of Kathakali. Dancers adorned in huge skirts and headdress with their faces covered with a most intricate style of makeup take the stage and, accompanied by drums and singers, recreate the characters, drama, and moods of the great Hindu epics of the *Ramayana* and *Mahabharata.*

Kathakali dancers combine dance and drama to create one of the most entertaining forms of Indian dance.

In recent years Indian plays that are similar to plays performed in London or New York have begun to be performed, plays where the classical themes are replaced by social themes with an emphasis on dialogue rather than dance.

MUSIC

India also has a rich tradition of classical music played on unique Indian instruments and based on musical structures unlike anything else in the world. The ancient musical styles that developed as spiritual music in the Hindu temples have been mixed with secular music introduced from Persia and Central Asia by the Moguls. The result is two primary forms of classical Indian music—the Hindustani style played mostly in north India and the Carnatic style that developed in south India. Both styles are based on a melodic base called the raga backed by a rhythm cycle called the tala. There are ragas to express every mood, emotion, or occasion—there are even ragas for each part of the day. Within the structure of each raga, the musicians are free to exercise imagination and creativity, so no raga is ever played exactly the same.

There are hundreds of different kinds of Indian musical instruments. The oldest are the drums and gongs, and the drum called the tabla, capable of producing different pitches, is an essential part of Indian music today. Among the many Indian stringed instruments, the vina, widely played in Ashoka's time (200 B.C.) is still popular in southern India. The sitar and sarod are similar stringed instruments that produce complex and dream-like tones. The Western violin is also a common instrument used in performances of classical and modern Indian music. Indian wind instruments depend on finger holes rather then keys and include exotic sounding (to Western ears) reed pipes like the popular *shehnai*.

Music is a large part of Indian culture. Here, a man plays one of a variety of Indian instruments.

LITERATURE

The Vedas, originally written in Sanskrit around 1500 B.C., existed much earlier as an oral tradition. The Rig-Veda, the oldest text, consists of 1,028 hymns in praise of the gods of nature. The four Vedas were originally considered to be the total of all knowledge. The Vedas are often hard to understand, but around 500 B.C. their lessons and stories were retold by the author Vyasa in his epic poems named the *Mahabharata* and *Ramayana*, making them more accessible to the people. One part in particular of the *Mahabharata*, the *Bhagavad Gita*, encapsulates Hindu philosophy. These stories have maintained their popular appeal through the ages, and dance-dramas based on these books are a major form of entertainment in India today.

Between the ancient texts and India's many respected modern authors, the subcontinent has produced a vast amount of literature, much of which remains unknown to

CLASSICAL INDIAN MUSIC, THE BEATLES, AND CALIFORNIA

The sitar is considered the finest instrument in the rarified world of classical Indian music, best compared, not in sound but in importance, to a combination of the grand piano and violin in Western symphonic music. Ravi Shankar is widely considered to be the world's foremost sitar player and interpreter of Indian classical music. In the 1960s, word of Shankar's skill reached the Beatles and they became his students. As a result, strains of Indian classical music have found their way into rock and roll.

When he was seventy-three and still giving performances in places like Carnegie Hall, Shankar moved with his family to San Diego county in southern California. His teenage daughter, Anoushka, is an honor student there and a serious musician in her own right. She is a devoted student of the sitar—she has the best teacher in the world—but she is also a fan of Metallica, Madonna, Marley, and Mozart. Will Anoushka take Indian classical music somewhere it has never gone before?

Indian musician Ravi Shankar is known worldwide for his expertise in playing the sitar.

the world at large. Courtly tales and poetry from the Mogul era, Tamil and Telugu poetry from the south of India, and Hindi novels are just a few examples of well-developed literary forms that are virtually unknown in the West. One Indian whose work has reached a broader audience is the poet, dramatist, and artist Rabindranath Tagore of Bengal. In 1913 Tagore won the Nobel Prize in literature for his collection of poems, *Gitanjali*. Gandhi called him Guru-Dev ("Divine Teacher"), and Stanley Wolpert, a foremost authority on India, said of Tagore, "He was India's greatest modern artist, transcending all bonds of birth and region or nation to dwell on the highest plain of art, where the most beautiful products of creative spirits from all climes and times inspire one another in the only truly universal 'language.'"[9]

The novels of many modern Indian writers are now available to English speakers. The best-known modern authors of Indian heritage are R. K. Narayan, V. S. Naipaul, A. Roy, and Salman Rushdie. Rushdie is also known for being the object of a Muslim *fatwa* (death sentence) that resulted from what Iranian Islamic leaders perceived as an anti-Muslim tone in one of his novels.

Indian author Rabindranath Tagore, winner of the 1913 Nobel Prize in literature, impressed the world with his poems and plays, and is still revered today.

SPORTS

Field hockey, soccer (called football in India and much of the rest of the world), cricket, basketball, volleyball, and local varieties of wrestling are popular sports in India's urban areas, with field hockey and cricket coming the closest to being the national sports. Tennis, golf, skiing, and yachting are popular with the more affluent. Indian teams have been world champions in field hockey, have won the Davis Cup in tennis, and have done well internationally in cricket and soccer. There are few professional athletes in India, however, and the government is far behind other countries in supporting sports. Consequently, India generally has not done well in the Olympics.

CLOTHING

In India, like other places, clothing can be an art form. Color and form of clothing is of importance to both men and women in India.

Indian women are well known for their graceful and colorful saris. The sari is a single rectangular piece of cloth fifteen to eighteen feet in length. The style, color, and texture of the fabric varies widely, and it can be made of cotton, silk, or a synthetic material. This graceful attire can fit any woman, and depending on how it is worn it can accentuate or conceal. The sari can be worn in several ways, and the way it is worn as well as its color and texture reveal much about the status, age, occupation, region, and religion of a woman. The fitted short blouse worn under a sari is called a *choli*. In some areas, especially in Rajasthan, women wear a pleated skirt with the *choli* in addition to a sari. In Kashmir and Punjab, as well as other parts of India, women often wear pajama-like pants called *salwars* and a long, loose tunic known as a *kameez*.

Indian men are more inclined to wear Western attire, and trousers and shirts are especially common in the cities. In villages, however, men are still more comfortable in traditional attire. *Kurtas* are collarless tunic shirts that can be simple or elaborately embroidered. *Lungis* and *dhotis* are short lengths of material worn like a sarong or pulled up between the legs. In many regions men wear a variety of colorful turbans ranging from the long, loose, colorful turbans of Rajasthanis to the carefully starched turbans of Sikhs.

INDIAN FIGHTER KITES

Indians are avid kite flyers, and they definitely take kite flying into the realm of sport. Every afternoon, the skies over the cities and towns are filled with flitting, dancing kites of every color as groups of kite flyers crowd the rooftops. Indians take a very active approach to kite flying and have perfected single-string kite maneuverability to a degree that has to be seen to be believed. A skilled flyer can dive one of these kites straight toward the ground and at the last possible instant, with a flick of the wrist, turn the kite to climb rapidly back into the sky.

What makes one of these highly controllable kites a "fighter" is powdered glass glued onto the string near the kite. The object is to get the kite to drag this part of the string across an opponent's string, instantly cutting the opponent's string. Of course, the opponent knows how to slack the string at the right moment so it won't be cut in two, and then immediately counterattack. Kite fighting gets serious. Sometimes entire villages challenge each other, and considerable sums are wagered on the outcome. Judges make sure that no flyer is using too long a cutting section on his string and that no pushing or shoving takes place up on the rooftops.

Indian women, wearing traditional saris, carry water.

INDIAN FOOD AND SPICES

Indians consider food an important part of their culture, and Indian food is as diverse as India's culture, geography, and climate. Indians believe that food influences behavior, attitudes, and health.

Indian food is rich and varied, and each region has its own specialties. Indian cuisine has been influenced by Hindu and Muslim traditions as well as by Portuguese, Persian, and British cooking styles and ingredients. Though most Hindus are vegetarians, their religion does not specifically forbid eating meat other than beef, and many Hindus eat pork,

A great variety of spices, such as these displayed in a Punjabi spice shop, are used in Indian cooking.

chicken, and fish. Muslim culture, on the other hand, has always included meats except pork. In addition, most Indians ascribe specific outcomes to eating certain foods. For example, meat and alcohol are believed to cause laziness and greed; rich and oily foods produce a quick temper and a love for luxury; and milk products, fresh vegetables, and fruits calm the body and sharpen the mind.

Certain ingredients are important in all Indian cooking: spices, legumes, and milk products like ghee (clarified butter), yogurt, and curds. Spices are the most well-known feature of Indian cooking. To Indians, spices are necessary not only for flavor but also for health. An entire system of ancient medicine, known as *ayurveda,* was developed around the health benefits of spices. The most frequently used spices in Indian food include pepper, fenugreek, clove, asafoetida, cinnamon, turmeric, ginger, cardamom, and coriander. Curries are made with various combinations of these spices. Legumes, including dal (lentils), peas, and beans, form the major source of protein for vegetarians. Yogurt and ghee are believed to be the favorite foods of Krishna, and these and other milk products form an essential part of the Indian diet. Yogurt neutralizes the effect of hot chilies and is consumed plain, salted, or sweetened, and it is cooked into various dishes and used in desserts.

In south India, most people are vegetarians, and rice is their staple grain. South Indian food is usually roasted or steamed, seldom greasy. Coconut is an important ingredient and is used in everything from curried vegetables and thick stews to dal dishes and rice pancakes (*dosas*). Most Indians like their food spicy hot, but the south is known for having the hottest dishes in all of India.

Northern Indians eat more meat and, though a lot of rice is consumed, griddle-cooked flat breads (chapatis and rotis) are the primary source of grain. Frying is more commonly used in the north than in the south, and curries, lentil dishes, curds and chutney are likely to appear at each meal. Muslim kitchens often have a clay oven called a tandoor that is used to prepare delicious tandoori rotis and chicken.

Indians love sweets, and they especially enjoy desserts based on milk products and sugar flavored with coconut, rose, chopped nuts, or cardamom. The poetic-sounding names of these sweets are known to every Indian: *rasagulla, gulab-jammuns, rasamalai, shahi tukra, kulfi,* and *kheer.* In the south, where the food is famously hot, even some desserts are made with hot chilies.

Many Indians are fond of chewing betel leaves after a meal. A betel leaf, called pan, is folded around chopped betel nuts, lime paste, and spices and slowly chewed. It is easy to spot a pan chewer because the juices stain the mouth a deep red. Many chew pan with tobacco and as a result become addicted to it.

Traditionally, Indians eat sitting on the floor and use the fingers of their right hand instead of forks and knives. In the south, many Indians prefer to eat their food from banana leaves, while in the north metal plates are preferred. Food from another person's plate or sips from another's glass are considered impure actions, and this taboo has been credited with helping to avoid disease epidemics.

FESTIVALS AND HOLIDAYS

Indians love to celebrate, and the calendar year is studded with a bewildering array of occasions for celebration. Most Indian festivals and holidays are religious in nature, and some events are celebrated by several different religions. There are also national and secular holidays and special days to honor married couples, brothers and sisters, ancestors, and parents.

A Hindu holy festival, many of which last for several days.

Many Indian festivals last a week or ten days, begin with fasting and end with feasting, and are accompanied by a fair or cultural performance. A few of India's more notable festivals and holidays are Holi, an exuberant, colorful end-of-winter celebration; Ganesh Chaturthi, dedicated to the popular elephant-headed Ganesh; Buddha Jayanti, which celebrates Buddha's birth and enlightenment; Id al Fitr, the Muslim celebration of the end of the Ramadan fasting; Christmas; Diwali, a festival of lights to guide Rama on his way home; Pongol, a Tamil end-of-harvest festival; and Janmashtami, which celebrates the birth of Krishna.

THE COMPLEXITIES AND CHALLENGES OF MODERN INDIA

6

India today has one foot in the past and one in the future. Indian society is now, as it has been for most of its existence, one of extreme contrasts and contradictions. The ancient religious-cultural caste system continues to influence the way society is organized even as modern influences are changing it. Three out of four Indians live in villages, and many of them are discovering free enterprise and new political and social concepts for the first time, often by watching one of the country's fifty cable television channels. Two of the country's important energy sources are nuclear power plants and dried cow dung. Over 60 percent of the population cannot read, yet India's pool of scientific and technical workers is the eighth largest in the world. Indian-built rockets have placed Indian-built satellites in orbit, only the seventh country to accomplish this feat, while about 40 percent of Indian villages lack electricity. Indian industry produces modern cars, aircraft, electronic equipment, and military weapons, but most people still cook on heat-wasting traditional stoves.

AN ECONOMY IN TRANSITION

India remains primarily an agricultural country with over two-thirds of the people engaged in farming. As recently as the middle of the twentieth century, however, parts of India faced famine anytime the monsoons failed to deliver the needed rains. Since independence, the introduction of intensive scientific farming methods has allowed farmers to increase yields even in off-years to the point where India now grows enough grain to feed the nation, maintain a surplus, and sell rice to other countries. India has been self-sufficient

Indians work in the paddy fields of east India. The Indian economy depends heavily on agriculture, and rice is one of the country's main crops.

in grain production since 1980 and has become the world's second largest exporter of rice (after Thailand).

India has a mixed economy. Most of the agriculture and many industries and businesses are owned privately, but other parts of the economy are owned and operated by the government, including weapons, mining, transport, communications, electricity, and power. Important industries include mining (iron ore, coal, bauxite, copper, mica, chromium, gold, and silver); cotton, silk, and wool textiles; chemicals; petroleum refining; sugar; leather products; vegetable oils; paper; and electronic equipment. Indian-made software is a growing segment of the economy.

The economy is also mixed in that it has characteristics of both underdeveloped and developed countries. India's exports have steadily grown, but it still imports more than it exports. The national currency, the rupee, is weak in world markets. The infrastructure of roads, railways, and seaports is well developed, but the telephone and postal service are inadequate for the needs of a modern country. India meets 70 percent of its energy needs through indigenous production, but it still must import significant quantities of oil.

During the 1980s and 1990s, India opened up its industry to foreign investment. That, along with other economic changes, caused the rapid growth of a Western-style market-driven economy. One result of this is the creation of a sizeable middle class. By the end of 1999, India's middle class numbered almost 250 million people, roughly the size of the entire population of the United States. Yet about 350 million Indians still live in poverty.

One of the economic changes that led to the growth of India's middle class was the removal of most import and price controls in 1993, originally intended to protect Indian manufacturers. Today, virtually anything from French-made perfume to American sneakers can be found in Indian department stores. Even that most American of institutions, McDonald's, has arrived in India, and now middle-class Indians can lunch on Maharajah Macs made with mutton instead of beef.

If India's economic managers are successful in modernizing India's economy, India will continue to make progress toward its primary economic goals of economic growth and reduction of poverty. Even with good plans and policies, lack of national unity due to squabbling political parties makes progress difficult.

India's first McDonald's opened in October 1996.

GOVERNMENT IN INDIA TODAY

India is a federal republic with twenty-six states and six territories governed by a constitutional democracy. Following the British model, India's federal government consists of a parliament with two houses. The prime minister is elected by the parliament, and the president is elected by popular vote. But these simple facts do not do justice to the spectacle of government in the world's largest democracy. Dozens of parties and hundreds of languages make the process of Indian government loud, colorful, and slow. Disagreements between factions have already produced one period in which constitutional freedoms were suspended (the "Emergency" under Indira Gandhi, 1975–1977), and the depth of these disagreements causes many observers to worry that democracy may not survive in India.

Indians, however, have a deep faith in democracy even as they are profoundly dissatisfied with politics. It is common for newspapers in India to express doubt that the country can hold together as a nation-state, although the overwhelming majority of Indians do not want the country to dissolve into smaller independent states in the manner of the old Union of Soviet Socialist Republics. According to a 1997 survey conducted by the weekly news magazine *India Today,* Indians are wary of politicians, police, and government bureaucracy. "People are appalled," stated the article that accompanied the survey, "by government unresponsiveness and corruption. Not surprisingly, corruption, unemployment, and rising prices rank high in people's concerns, overshadowing caste and community tensions."[10]

Despite its faith in democracy, India is engulfed by self-doubt over its political system. Though national pride is strong and there is a commitment to keeping India together, Indian society has not yet succeeded in dissolving the fragmenting forces of caste, religion, and region.

THE CASTE SYSTEM TODAY

Based on ancient Indo-Aryan social structures, the caste system divides society into distinct social groups. Despite some changes in the caste system, in contemporary India most social relations and many economic and political exchanges continue to maintain it. While the caste system provides order and a prescribed code of conduct for all, it also creates vast social inequalities that result in exploitation of the lower castes. At the top of the caste ladder are the Brahmins, the elite of Hinduism, and below them are the merchants, soldiers, and three thousand other castes and subcastes. At the very bottom are the outcastes, known as the Untouchables, including scavengers, sweepers, and butchers. Gandhi called them harijan, meaning children of God.

The constitution of India legally abolished untouchability in 1955 and set up a list called the "Scheduled Tribes and Backward Classes." The legislation targets the harijan and other "scheduled castes" for special education, employment, and welfare services to help integrate them into society—an Indian affirmative action program.

For at least some harijans, the program is working. One of the judges on India's Supreme Court, K. Ramaswamy, was born an Untouchable and grew up on the street. While many people of his caste are sweeping streets, Judge Ramaswamy is working to sweep away injustice.

Untouchables walk the streets. Despite changes in the caste system, most Indians observe its rigid social control.

"My proudest moment," he says, "is when I wipe away the tears of a man who needs justice by rendering justice."[11]

The political awakening of the lower castes has also caused political turmoil, and in six years during the 1990s, that turmoil toppled five different governments. These people who have traditionally been excluded from politics in India are voting in growing numbers, and several political parties have sprung up to represent these castes. As an example of the trend, a study by the Center for the Study of Developing Societies found "people from formerly untouchable castes who said they were members of political parties rose from 13 percent in 1971 to 19 percent in 1996. . . . [T]he percentage of very poor people who believe voting makes a difference rose from 38 percent in 1971 to 51 percent in 1996."[12] The poorest Indians are now more likely to vote than the richest ones, just the opposite of voting trends in the United States and Western Europe.

In April 1999, the Bahujan Samaj Party, a small political party of the lower castes, brought down the ruling coalition led by the Hindu nationalist Bharatiya Janata Party (known as the BJP) by casting the deciding ballot in a vote of confidence. The mighty BJP, the party that had aggressively sponsored India's latest round of nuclear tests next to the Pakistani border, was toppled by the party of some of India's poorest people.

INDIANS TODAY

At the end of the twentieth century, the typical Indian is likely to be Hindu, have an annual income equivalent to about five hundred U.S. dollars, and live in a village. Three-quarters of Indians live in the more than five hundred thousand villages dotting the nation's hills and countryside. Even for many who work and live in the cities, the village remains the focus of their social lives because their families and friends remain there.

In India, daily life is centered on family much more than in Western countries. Despite Western influences and urbanization, the traditional household remains the primary social force in the lives of most Indians. Traditional households consist of a senior couple, their married sons with their wives and children, any unmarried children, and possibly other relatives. All live in a single house, cook at a single hearth, spend from a single purse, worship at a single altar, and obey the single authority of the eldest male.

A woman living in a traditional Indian village draws water from the village well.

India has been and still is a patriarchal society. All males are co-owners of the family's assets, each with an equal share regardless of age; village women seldom share in property ownership. Modern laws have established equal property rights for women, but there has been little practical change in the villages.

Most Indians consider marriage the most honorable way to live as an adult. The vast majority of marriages are pre-arranged by the families of the prospective spouses and in-volve lengthy negotiations and approvals from both families and consultations with astrologers. Even today marriages between people of different castes are rare. In traditional In-dian marriages, the married couple generally does not share emotional closeness until after years of marriage, if then, and divorce is very rare.

Many urban Indians are caste-conscious and likely to be married by arrangement, but in the city an arranged mar-riage is more likely to begin with an advertisement in a spe-cial matrimonial section of a newspaper. Furthermore, city Indians are more likely to be college educated, make more money, and be somewhat more influenced by Western styles and values than village Indians.

THE STATUS OF WOMEN IN INDIA

Indian women are equal to men by law, but those laws have effect mostly in the cities, where only a quarter of India's women live. Even among city women, arranged marriages within the same caste remain the rule, as does male authority over the family. There are regional exceptions, as in Kerala in the south and Manipur in the east, where even village women enjoy considerable freedom and equality with men.

In the cities, society is changing very fast, and female professionals are a relatively new but growing phenomenon. Economic independence and the women's liberation movement imported from the West have given urban Indian women new freedom and power.

The most extreme of gender inequalities that were prevalent as recently as the first half of the twentieth century are now almost nonexistent. Purdah, the custom of women not being seen in public without having their entire bodies and faces covered, is no longer practiced except in the strictest Muslim households. Child brides are illegal. Suttee, the practice of a widow being expected to throw herself on her husband's funeral pyre, has disappeared.

Still, India is a long way from achieving gender equality. One of the most emotionally charged women's issues in modern India is the phenomena of "bride burning" and "dowry murders." A dowry is a sum of money or jewelry paid by the bride's family to the groom, and even though demanding a dowry is now against the law, in traditional arranged marriages they are still almost always paid. The trouble starts when dowry payments are stopped or a woman fails to produce a son. Authorities believe that in Delhi alone, more than a thousand young brides are burned to death each year, either as an act of suicide because they can no longer tolerate the physical and psychological abuse of their husbands and their families or as an act of murder by mothers-in-law, husbands, and other in-laws who stage it to look like an accidental burning. Women's groups, lawyers, and others are attempting to have more of these cases investigated and to pass stronger laws against the dowry.

Muslim women walk in public, completely covered. Purdah is still practiced in the strictest Muslim households.

Environmental Challenges

Like most habitable places on earth, population growth in India is bringing humanity into direct conflict and competition

INDIA'S FIRST WOMAN IN SPACE

Kalpana Chawla was a thirty-five-year-old scientist when, as a member of an international team of astronauts, she went into space for a fifteen-day mission on the space shuttle in 1997. Her primary task was to release a $10 million solar physics satellite from the space shuttle's bay.

According to *India Today Online,* Ms. Chawla found that experiencing zero gravity was more profound than she had expected it to be. "One of the strangest things is that when I was about to sleep, I realized that I was only aware of my thoughts. Because you are weightless, you don't feel your legs or your body. In a sense then, you are just your intelligence. It's amazing you can't feel anything but your consciousness."

Weightlessness was only the beginning of the effect space flight had on India's first woman astronaut. According to the scientist, the experience changed her whole outlook on life: "I really feel responsible for the earth now. There are so many people who are arguing or fighting over issues which don't have much relevance. . . . It's like being in the whirlpools which are always present behind a little rock near a river. We seem to be living in these little whirlpools and forget that there is the whole river. . . . We should take time to look at the big picture."

with many classes of plants and animals. In India, however, the flora and fauna are especially rich and the population growth is particularly great, so the problem is greater and more urgent than in most other countries. There is constant pressure to turn forests and wetlands into more living and farming space for humans. Species diversity, both for animals and plants, is declining at an alarming rate.

The most serious environmental problems in India today are deforestation, soil erosion, overgrazing, desertification, air pollution from industrial effluents and vehicle emissions (Delhi has the fourth worst air pollution in the world), and water pollution from raw sewage and runoff of agricultural pesticides (only a few parts of the country have safe drinking water). The government is working hard on many fronts to reverse the downward trends in India's environment, but the immense population is overstraining natural resources and still growing fast.

NUCLEAR POWER

India began generating electricity from a nuclear reactor in the 1960s, but the country's atomic energy program had another goal too. India tested its first atom bomb in 1974, and following that test remained quiet about its nuclear capabilities for more than two decades. Then in 1998 the recently elected government of the Indian nationalist JPT Party ordered new nuclear tests to be conducted in the Thar Desert near the Pakistan border.

To many observers, the location and the timing of the tests (fighting in Kashmir was escalating) seemed calculated to threaten their neighbor. Indian officials, however, denied this. T. P. Srinivasan, an Indian diplomat to the United States, said about his nation's recent atomic tests, "This is a question of a major country having the technological capability to look after itself. In fact, every major country in the world today either has nuclear weapons or it has a security agreement from some other nuclear weapons state. So we have chosen an independent path."[13]

There are reasons to fear a nuclear catastrophe on the subcontinent. Both India and Pakistan now have nuclear warheads, both have shown that they have the missiles and aircraft to deliver these weapons, the two countries are filled

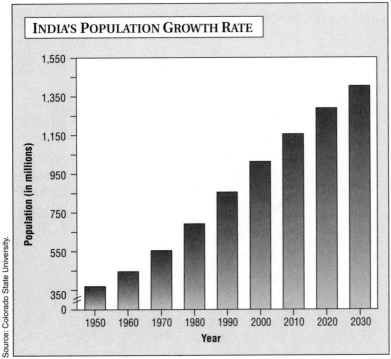

with distrust for each other, and both have large populations that would suffer greatly in even a limited nuclear attack. Many people on both sides oppose any use of nuclear weapons, but some powerful forces appear to have taken the opposite position. Zia Mian, a Pakistani-born nuclear expert living in the United States, believes there are generals on both sides who think they would become national heroes by eradicating the other country. According to Mian, "A day might well come when these people would say, 'Let's get it over with forever, once and for all, no matter what the cost.'"[14]

Some Indians are eager to see their nation recognized as a world power, and having nuclear weapons is viewed by many as a way to gain the international respect they desire for their country. The concern that many have, both inside and outside the subcontinent, is that this new nuclear face-off is different from and possibly more dangerous than the old Cold War between the United States and the Soviet Union. The question now is who will gain the political power in India—those who passionately support the new nuclear status and are willing to use atomic weapons, or those who just as passionately oppose them.

CONTINUING FRICTION WITH PAKISTAN

Beginning with the violence that followed partition of the subcontinent into Pakistan and India, the two countries have

India's military has grown steadily. Pictured here is military equipment in New Delhi.

been distrustful neighbors. Hostility has erupted in wars in 1948, 1965, and 1971, and fighting has been almost continuous along the border in the mountains above Kashmir. At partition, sovereignty over Kashmir was disputed by both sides. Though most of that territory was eventually occupied by India, the dispute has never been resolved, and military actions have continued there almost without stop for fifty years.

Kashmir is a beautiful mountainous region in the northwest of India, although Pakistanis would say it is in the northeast of Pakistan. In 1947, Kashmir had a mostly Muslim population and a Hindu ruler or Maharajah. With independence and partition in effect, the Maharajah was given the choice of going with Pakistan or India. In October 1947 the indecisive Maharajah finally chose to join India, and, as a consequence, the first India-Pakistan war broke out the following year. The United Nations stepped in with international troops and stopped the conflict.

Kashmir has remained a point of disagreement. Battles occur almost daily at high altitudes and in freezing temperatures. Every year many soldiers on both sides die fighting for control of the glacier that marks the current border. Both sides claim the other is the aggressor and neither will yield to United Nations demands for a cease-fire.

India is a fully militarized country with 1.3 million soldiers, which gives it the fourth largest army in the world, after China, the United States, and Russia. So far, the Indian army has fought with conventional weapons, but now that both Pakistan and India have nuclear weapons, the bitter rivalry between these two countries glows with a new level of danger.

A GROWING POPULATION

India's population is huge, and the rate at which it is growing threatens to wipe out every gain the country makes. India has worked hard to reduce its growth rate, and today it is holding steady at about 2 percent, roughly half of what it was back in 1951 when Nehru started the first family planning program of any developing nation. With a population close to 1 billion, however, 2 percent is still a lot—another 18 million new mouths to feed each year. To put that in perspective, 18 million more people is like adding more than half of the present population of Canada every twelve months to a country that is only a third the size of Canada.

A census taker talks to an Indian family living in a slum of New Delhi. Much of India's large population lives in poverty.

HUNGERING FOR PEACE

The diverse people of India know that they need peace to attain the prosperity, spirituality, and cultural expression that once made the subcontinent one of the greatest lands on earth. Yet with India's population growth, threats of another war with Pakistan, quarreling political parties, illiteracy, unemployment, and many other problems, now more than ever India needs to heed the words of the great Mahatma Gandhi:

> If we are to reach real peace in this world and if we are to carry on a real war against war, we shall have to begin with children; and if they will grow up in their natural innocence, we won't have to struggle; we won't have to pass fruitless idle resolutions, but we shall go from love to love and peace to peace, until at last all the corners of the world are covered with that peace and love for which consciously or unconsciously the whole world is hungering.[15]

FACTS ABOUT INDIA

GEOGRAPHY

Location: Southern Asia, bordering the Arabian Sea and the Bay of Bengal, between Bangladesh and Pakistan

Total area (including lakes and bays): 1.27 million square miles (3.29 million square km)

Comparative area: Slightly more than one-third the size of the United States

Total land boundaries: 8,814 miles (14,103 km); by country: Bangladesh 2,533 miles (4,053 km); Bhutan 375 miles (605 km); Burma 914 miles (1,463 km); China 2,112 miles (3,380 km); Nepal 1,056 miles (1,690 km); Pakistan 1,820 miles (2,912 km)

Coastline: 4,375 miles (7,000 km)

International disputes: boundaries with Bangladesh and China; status of Kashmir with Pakistan; water-sharing problems with downstream riparians, Bangladesh over the Ganges River, and Pakistan over the Indus River

Climate: varies from tropical monsoon in south to freezing in north

Terrain: upland plain (Deccan Plateau) in south, flat to rolling plain along Ganges River, deserts in west, Himalayas in north

Highest point: Kanchenjunga Peak 28,208 feet (8,598 meters)

Capital: New Delhi

Natural resources: coal (fourth-largest reserves in the world), iron ore, manganese, mica, bauxite, titanium ore, chromite, natural gas, diamonds, petroleum, limestone

Land use: arable land: 55 percent; permanent crops: 1 percent; meadows and pastures: 4 percent; forest and woodland: 23 percent; other: 17 percent

PEOPLE

Population (1999): 960 million

GOVERNMENT

Type: A parliamentary democracy; member of the British Commonwealth of Nations

Parliament: consists of Rajya Sabha (Council of States) and Lok Sabha (House of Representatives)

Head of state: president; appointed by both houses of the parliament

Head of government: prime minister; leader of the majority party of the Lok Sabha

NOTES

INTRODUCTION: INDIA: "LAND OF WONDERS"

1. Mark Twain, *Following the Equator, and AntiImperialist Essays (1897, 1901, 1905).* New York: Oxford University Press, 1997, p. 537.

CHAPTER 2: ROOTS: THREE THOUSAND YEARS OF INDIAN CIVILIZATION

2. Quoted in A. L. Basham, *The Wonder That Was India.* New York: Grove Press, 1954, p. 88.

CHAPTER 3: FROM BRITISH COLONY TO THE WORLD'S LARGEST DEMOCRACY

3. Quoted in David Carroll, *The Taj Mahal.* New York: Newsweek Books, 1972, p. 130.

4. Richard Attenborough, ed., *The Words of Gandhi.* New York: Newmarket Press, 1982, p. 44.

5. Attenborough, *The Words of Gandhi,* p. 18.

6. Quoted in Attenborough, *The Words of Gandhi,* p. 9.

CHAPTER 4: SPIRITUAL AND ETHNIC DIVERSITY

7. Mohandas K. Gandhi, *An Autobiography, or the Story of My Experiments with Truth.* New York: Greenleaf Books, 1927, p. 615.

8. Quoted in Ainslie T. Embree, ed., *The Hindu Tradition.* New York: Random House, 1966, p. 21.

CHAPTER 5: ART AND CULTURE

9. Stanley Wolpert, *India.* Berkeley: University of California Press, 1991, p. 159.

CHAPTER 6: THE COMPLEXITIES AND CHALLENGES OF MODERN INDIA

10. *India Today,* "50 Years Later," July 18, 1997. www.india-today.com.

11. Quoted in Geoffrey C. Ward, "India," *National Geographic,* May 1997, p. 37.

12. *New York Times,* "India's Poorest Are Becoming Its Loudest," April 25, 1999.

13. Quoted in *San Diego Union-Tribune,* "An Interview with T. P. Sreenivasan," July 5, 1998, p. G-5.

14. Quoted in Amitav Ghosh, "Countdown: Why Can't Every Country Have the Bomb?" *The New Yorker,* October 26, 1998, p. 195.

15. Quoted in Attenborough, *The Words of Gandhi,* p. 101.

CHRONOLOGY

B.C.
2500
Planned cities appear in the Indus Valley

1000
Aryans expand into the Ganges River plain

800
Mahabharata and first version of *Ramayana* composed

544
Buddha's enlightenment

327
Alexander the Great of Macedonia enters India

322
Rise of the Mauryas; Chandragupta establishes first Indian empire

272
Ashoka's reign begins

A.D.
380
Chandragupta II comes to power; India's classical age

476
Birth of Indian astronomer Aryabhatta

1288
Marco Polo visits India

1398
Timur invades India

1498
First voyage of Vasco da Gama

1510
Portuguese capture Goa

1526
Babur establishes the Mogul Dynasty

1600
British East India Company starts business in Bengal

1628
Shah Jahan proclaimed Mogul emperor

1631
Death of Shah Jahan's wife Mumtaz Mahal; construction of the Taj Mahal begun

1658
Aurangzeb proclaimed Mogul emperor

1686
English at war with Moguls

1757
British victory at the Battle of Plassey

1772
Warren Hastings appointed governor of Bengal, and in 1774, Governor-General of India

1784
Pitt's India Act

1848–1849
Anglo-Sikh wars end with British annexing Punjab as Sikhs defeated

1857
The Sepoy Mutiny

1858
British Crown takes over Indian government from East India Company

1877
Queen of England proclaimed empress of India

1885
First meeting of Indian National Congress

1906
Formation of Muslim League

1920
Mahatma Gandhi leads Congress Party, begins noncooperation campaign

1923
Hindu-Muslim riots

1929
British promise independence for India; Jawaharlal Nehru hoists Indian flag at Lahore

1930
Civil disobedience movement continues; Gandhi's salt tax protest

1947
Mountbatten announces plan for partition of India; India gains independence; Jawaharlal Nehru becomes first Indian prime minister; Maharajah of Kashmir agrees to join India

1948
Assassination of Mahatma Gandhi in New Delhi; India and Pakistan at war over Kashmir; United Nations–monitored cease-fire ends fighting January 1949

1949
New constitution of India adopted and signed

1952
First general election; Indian atomic energy establishment set up in Bombay

1955
Chinese troops enter India's Garhwal district in Uttar Pradesh; Untouchability Act passed

1959
Dalai Lama flees from Tibet to refuge in India; fighting between India and China breaks out

1961
Portuguese return Goa to India

1962
India and China at war from October 1962 to June 1965

1964

Jawaharlal Nehru dies; Lal Bahadur Shastri becomes prime minister; Pakistani tanks penetrate India, beginning new Pakistan-India war

1966

Tashkent Conference between Pakistani and Indian leaders; Lal Bahadur Shastri dies; Indira Gandhi becomes prime minister

1971

India and Pakistan at war again; East Pakistan becomes Bangladesh

1972

Pakistan and India sign Simla Accord; monsoon failure causes drought

1974

Underground nuclear device detonated at Pokhran

1975

First Indian satellite *Aryabhatta* launched from a Soviet missile

1975–1976

Emergency Proclamation, civil liberties suspended over political dissension

1977

First non-Congress government, led by Morarji Desai

1979

Bhaskara, India's second satellite, launched from a Soviet cosmodrome; Morarji Desai resigns after split in Janata Party

1980

Indira Gandhi becomes prime minister again

1983

India wins the Cricket World Cup; Indira Gandhi imposes president's rule on Punjab

1984

Indian army storms Golden Temple in Amritsar, killing hundreds of people; Indira Gandhi assassinated in Delhi;

her son Rajiv Gandhi sworn in as prime minister; India's biggest industrial disaster—Bhopal poison gas tragedy

1988
First Indian satellite (*Insat-IC*) launched with Indian rocket

1989
Congress Party loses and V. P. Singh becomes prime minister

1991
Rajiv Gandhi assassinated; Congress wins; Narasimha Rao becomes prime minister

1993
Hindu-Muslim riots in Bombay

1996
BJP's Atal Behari Vajpayee becomes prime minister

1997
Nation celebrates 50 years of independence; Mother Teresa dies; Gujral government falls as Congress withdraws support

1998
Indian chess master Vishwanathan Anand wins the Super Grand Master Title; BJP-led alliance government is sworn in; Atal Behari Vajpayee becomes prime minister; India conducts three underground nuclear tests at the Pokhran Range in Rajasthan

Suggestions for Further Reading

Richard Attenborough, ed., *The Words of Gandhi.* New York: Newmarket Press, 1982. Inspiring and revealing, this small book is a glimpse into the great man's soul.

A. L. Basham, *The Wonder That Was India.* New York: Grove Press, 1954. For those who want all the details told in an interesting style, Basham takes a close look at India up to the Mogul period.

David Carroll, *The Taj Mahal.* New York: Newsweek Books, 1972. Not just a detailed examination of the intriguing history of the Taj Mahal but also an exciting look into Mogul India and the time of the British Raj.

George Constable, ed., *India—Library of Nations.* New York: Time-Life Books, 1986. A quick look at India. Constable includes some topics not covered in other books and many excellent photographs.

Irfan Habib, *An Atlas of the Mughal Empire.* Delhi: Oxford University Press, 1982. This detailed and well-illustrated book describes all the glory, art, and intrigue of the Moguls.

Stanley Wolpert, *India.* Berkeley: University of California Press, 1991. Wolpert, a professor of Indian history at UCLA, presents an all-around reference book with especially good sections on arts and sciences, society, and politics.

Websites

India-Connect (www.indiaconnect.com). This website is a search engine for all things Indian.

India Today (www.india-today.com). *India Today* is an illustrated weekly news magazine somewhat like *Time* or

Newsweek. It is an excellent source of up-to-the-minute information about modern India.

Welcome to India (www.welcometoindia.com). This is a fun site that serves as a good introduction to Indian culture.

WORKS CONSULTED

Jed Adams and Philip Whitehead, *The Dynasty: The Nehru-Gandhi Story*. New York: TV Books, 1998. The government during most of the 50+ years of Indian independence has been headed by a prime minister named Nehru or Gandhi. This is the intimate story of this close-knit family and how power has been used and abused in modern India.

Ainslie T. Embree, ed., *The Hindu Tradition*. New York: Random House, 1966. This book unravels the marvelous complexity and flexibility of the world's oldest living religion, the religion that is said to be all things to all people.

C. J. Fuller, *The Camphor Flame: Popular Hinduism and Society in India*. New York: Columbia University Press, 1992. This book examines the universal role in Indian life played by Hinduism. The caste system is revealed to be as influential as it has ever been despite laws and social changes that have caused expression of this fundamental aspect of the Hindu order to shift.

Mohandas K. Gandhi, *An Autobiography, or the Story of My Experiments with Truth*. New York: Greenleaf Books, 1927. The classic work about nonviolence as a politically powerful weapon; this book was cited by Martin Luther King Jr. as a major influence.

Salim Al-Din Quraishi, S. M. Burke, *The British Raj in India*. New York: Oxford University Press, 1997. This is a scholarly, detailed book about the Raj that considers the Indian and British viewpoints and finds faults and strengths in both.

Arthur Lall, *The Emergence of Modern India*. New York: Columbia University Press, 1981. This book provides a thorough consideration of nineteenth and twentieth century Indian history.

V. S. Naipaul, *An Area of Darkness*. New York: Penguin USA, 1992. A painfully honest look at India's inferiority complex resulting from British domination. Naipaul is an Indian living outside of India who, in this book, also considers his roots.

Richard F. Nyrop, *India, a Country Study.* 4th ed. Washington, DC: U.S. Government Printing Office, 1975. An overview of India with the most detail and thought devoted to political and economic issues of modern India.

Radhika Srinivasan, *India.* New York: Marshall Cavendish, 1993. A colorful book that provides unusual glimpses into the beauty of India and Indians not found in other books.

Emma Tarlo, *Clothing Matters: Dress and Identity in India.* Chicago: University of Chicago Press, 1996. Here are detailed descriptions of the wide spectrum of men's and women's clothing in the cultural and regional diversity of India and how a person's caste, economic position, and geographical origins are indicated by clothing.

Mark Twain, *Following the Equator, and AntiImperialist Essays (1897, 1901, 1905).* New York: Oxford University Press, 1997. A collection of essays by the famous American writer.

Stanley Wolpert, *A New History of India.* 5th ed. New York: Oxford University Press, 1997. Wolpert, a professor of Indian history at UCLA, presents the definitive book on India's past from prehistoric times to the present. This book offers a superior history of the Raj.

Internet Sources

World Wildlife Federation, *Species Diversity in India,* 1997. www.wcmc.org.uk/iglmc/main.html.

Periodicals

Amitav Ghosh, "Countdown:Why Can't Every Country Have the Bomb?" *The New Yorker,* October 26, 1998.

New York Times, "India's Poorest Are Becoming Its Loudest," April 25, 1999.

San Diego Union-Tribune, "An Interview with T. P. Sreenivasan," July 5, 1998.

Jean Schinto, "Imposter Poodles and Phantom Limbs—V. S. Ramachandran's Artful Brain," *San Diego Reader,* July 15, 1999.

Geoffrey C. Ward, "India," *National Geographic,* May 1997.

INDEX

Picture Credits

ABOUT THE AUTHOR

William Goodwin lives in San Diego. He is a graduate of the University of California at Los Angeles and has also undertaken graduate studies in biochemistry, education, and English. He writes in a variety of fields, including biotechnology, marketing/communications, young adult fiction and nonfiction, business, and education. He has taught high school sciences, owned and operated a boating school, written scripts for educational videos, and built a forty-three-foot sailboat. He has two teenagers, Gideon and Marilyn, and he travels through life with Donna, his best friend. Mr. Goodwin has traveled extensively in Asia and has made three trips to India.